"In a dynamic conversation (actually an e-
Preston Jones, the Christian history professor, and punk rocker Greg Graffin over matters of consequence, we see elements of Christian theism and scientific naturalism going head to head. I was drawn deeply into their intellectual volleys, their spiritual perspectives and their friendship. I also learned about books and issues that were new to me. This work is a model of civility on the part of both parties, and an enlightening one at that!"

**DAVID NAUGLE,** PROFESSOR OF PHILOSOPHY, DALLAS BAPTIST UNIVERSITY, AND AUTHOR OF *WORLDVIEW: THE HISTORY OF A CONCEPT*

"I've overheard numerous conversations but none as captivating as this. Greg Graffin and Preston Jones disagree agreeably while discussing the things that matter most. I learned from both, grew in appreciation for the creative music of Bad Religion and reflected on how better to flesh out my faith in a pluralistic world. I hope all my friends accept their invitation to listen in. This is a book that needs to be not just read, but discussed."

**DENIS D. HAACK,** DIRECTOR OF RANSOM FELLOWSHIP, EDITOR OF *CRITIQUE,* AND VISITING INSTRUCTOR IN PRACTICAL THEOLOGY, COVENANT SEMINARY

"A good spirited conversation can be very educational. It gives people the freedom to draw their own conclusions, which is usually more powerful than forcing one down the reader's throat. Preston Jones has 'authored' a great read simply by keeping the conversation true to what was 'said' via his e-mails with Bad Religion frontman Greg Graffin. This collection of back-and-forth debate concerning the worldviews of a naturalist and a Christian is fascinating and as compelling as a suspense novel, as educational as a college course and as relational as a blog. [Readers] will appreciate the frankness found inside this book."

**DOUG VAN PELT,** EDITOR OF *HM MAGAZINE,* AND AUTHOR OF *ROCK STARS ON GOD*

# IS BELIEF IN GOD GOOD, BAD OR IRRELEVANT?

## A PROFESSOR AND A PUNK ROCKER DISCUSS SCIENCE, RELIGION, NATURALISM & CHRISTIANITY

EDITED BY PRESTON JONES

An imprint of InterVarsity Press
Downers Grove, Illinois

*InterVarsity Press*
*P.O. Box 1400, Downers Grove, IL 60515-1426*
*World Wide Web: www.ivpress.com*
*E-mail: mail@ivpress.com*



*InterVarsity Press® is the book-publishing division of InterVarsity Christian Fellowship/USA®, a student movement active on campus at hundreds of universities, colleges and schools of nursing in the United States of America, and a member movement of the International Fellowship of Evangelical Students. For information about local and regional activities, write Public Relations Dept., InterVarsity Christian Fellowship/USA, 6400 Schroeder Rd., P.O. Box 7895, Madison, WI 53707-7895, or visit the IVCF website at <www.intervarsity.org>.*



*Cover Design: Matt Smith*
*Interior Design: Cindy Kiple*
*Images: Royalty Free/Corbis*

*ISBN-10: 0-8308-3377-3*
*ISBN-13: 978-0-8308-3377-1*

*Printed in the United States of America* ∞

**Library of Congress Cataloging-in-Publication Data**

*Jones, Preston, 1966-*
*Is belief in God good, bad, or irrelevant?: a professor and a punk*
*rocker discuss science, religion, naturalism, and Christianity / edited by Preston Jones.*
*p. cm.*
*E-mail correspondence between Preston Jones and Greg Graffin.*
*Includes bibliographical references. ISBN-13: 978-0-8308-3377-1 (pbk.: alk. paper) ISBN-10: 0-8308-3377-3 (pbk.: alk. paper) 1. Apologetics. 2. Jones, Preston, 1966- —Correspondence.*
*3. Graffin, Greg—Correspondence. I. Graffin, Greg. II. Title.*
*BT1103.J66 2006 261.2'1—dc22*

*2005034281*

**P** 17 16 15 14 13 12 11 10 9 8 7 6 5 4 3
**Y** 19 18 17 16 15 14 13 12 11 10 09 08 07 06

For Annemarie

and

Tory and Eric

*filii Dei vocabuntur*

They shall be called children of God

# CONTENTS

Acknowledgments 9

Introduction 13

THE DIALOGUE

Getting Acquainted 21

Inquisitions 24

Hating God 31

Odd Christians and Naturalism 34

The Tough World 40

Books 45

Theism Versus Naturalism 52

The End of the Tour 60

The Inevitability of People and Foundations for Morality 63

The Fall 78

Free Will 87

Freedom and Environment 95

Mystery 102

Fan Mail 118

Christianity and Violence 132

Proximate Versus Ultimate Meaning 137

Study Guide 147

Notes 159

About the Authors 165

# ACKNOWLEDGMENTS

Most of the correspondence that makes up Greg Graffin's portion of this book was written while Bad Religion was on its 2003 tour in the U.S. Southwest. Most of my notes were written at home, after work or on Saturdays. So thanks, most of all, to my wife and best friend, Anne, who let me do that. I also thank my colleagues, David Brisben, Robbie Castleman, Breck Castleman and Ed Klotz, who commented on the manuscript, as well as Mike Clawson and Juliana Vazquez for their very useful comments and criticisms. Thanks as well to Jenny Glass, an intelligent Bad Religion fan who wrote to Greg. Two of her letters are included in these pages. Of course, a one-sided conversation is dull, so I'm grateful to Greg, who challenged me to think.

For their comments on and criticisms of different parts of the manuscript, I am grateful to the following students: Carole Anderson, Kenneth Boggs, Laura Boyd, Andrew Bradford, Laura Burgess, Tim Chang, Lee Charles, Susan Crittenden, Mar Cruz, Snorri Danielsen, Andy Everding, Chris Fowler, Ethan Fowler, Todd Frazier, Lindsay Hamm, Adam Harbottle, Alex Heitz, Gabriel Herrera, Samal Jakobsen, Carole Johnson, Jennifer Johnson, Kandi Johnson, Ashley Kenline, Courtney Laufert, Sarah Lyman, Jared Mackall, Matt Menhennett, Mark Minnich, Sophie Morris, Mary Nazworth, Jill Neufeld, Bethany Nelson, Heidi Nightengale, Leah Olson, Carrie Peter, Nathan Piquard, Katie Radaker, Laura Ravenscroft, Peter Reither, Matthew Sample, Courtney Simmons, Lauren Staton, Stephanie Watkins and Daniel Wolfe. I also thank my teaching assistant, Ruby Vazquez, for her help with citations.

Finally, I am grateful to Al Hsu, my editor at IVP, whose patience, goodwill and professionalism are enviable.

**Naturalism:** The view that all phenomena can be explained in terms of natural causes and laws.

**Theism:** Belief in the existence of a god or gods.

—*American Heritage Dictionary*

I believe in God, the Father almighty,
creator of heaven and earth.
I believe in Jesus Christ, his only Son, our Lord.
He was conceived by the power of the Holy Spirit
and born of the Virgin Mary.
He suffered under Pontius Pilate,
was crucified, died, and was buried.
He descended into hell.
On the third day he rose again.
He ascended into heaven,
and is seated at the right hand of the Father.
He will come again to judge the living and the dead.
I believe in the Holy Spirit,
the holy catholic Church,
the communion of saints,
the forgiveness of sins,
the resurrection of the body,
and the life everlasting. Amen.

—The Apostles' Creed

# INTRODUCTION

In the summer of 1983 or '84, my best friend, John, and I returned to my house after a day at Parris Lake in Southern California. As soon as we walked in the door I turned on my radio, which was tuned to the station based at the University of Redlands. Simultaneously I hit the "play" and "record" buttons on the radio's cassette player. The station, KUOR, always had something cool on the air, something that couldn't be heard on any other station in San Bernardino, where John and I grew up. That evening, KUOR was playing punk, and one of the songs I recorded was titled (I thought) "Well Go Ahead and Die." It became my favorite eighties punk song. But I never knew who recorded it, and I never understood its lyrics, except for the line "Early man walked away, and Spider-Man's in control," which doesn't exactly make sense.

Fast-forward to 1994. I had been out of the Navy for four years and was working my way through a master's program at California State University, Sonoma. As had been the case since 1990, I was working as a counselor at a psychiatric facility. One evening at work a patient, whom I'll call Rob, was playing an album (this was before the CD era) that caught my attention. The music's driving bass and guitars, the harmony, the intelligent lyrics—it was all quite catchy. Rob, who himself was pretty bright, was playing Bad Religion's *Stranger Than Fiction*. The next day I bought my own copy—on cassette—and *Stranger Than Fiction* became something that helped Rob and me connect. Rob told me about Bad Religion's lead singer, who he said was a professor at Boston College. In the evenings when Rob and I would talk, he would analyze BR's lyrics, making philosophical connections among songs on different records.

Fast-forward again to 2001. I'm living in Dallas now, cleaning the bathroom at home and listening to another Bad Religion tape, *All Ages*, which I had bought a few years before but hadn't listened to very often. The next song came on, and I realized that my favorite eighties punk tune was by BR, whose sound had changed over the years. I also learned that the song's real title was "We're Only Gonna Die," and that the lyrics I thought were about Spider-Man actually said, "Early man walked away as modern man took control." Yes, all those years I had been mistakenly singing about an action hero.

***Father, can you hear me?***
***How have I let you down?***
***I curse the day that I was born,***
***And all the sorrow in this world. . . .***
***When all soldiers lay their weapons down,***
***Or when all kings and all queens relinquish their crowns,***
***Or when the only true messiah rescues us from ourselves . . .***
***It's easy to imagine there will be . . .***
***Sorrow, no more.***

**Greg Graffin, "Sorrow,"**
***The Process of Belief* (2002)**

Fast-forward one last time to early 2003. On the headmaster's desk at the Christian preparatory school where I was teaching was Bad Religion's new CD—modern technology at last!—*The Process of Belief*. The headmaster told me that his son, a college student in Maine, had recommended the CD to him, and he intended to play a couple BR songs to his theology students the next day. He wanted his students to think about the lyrics and reflect on how they would respond in conversation to a person who took BR's point of view. The following morning I heard "Sorrow," one of the best songs on *Process*, blaring from the classroom across the hall.

Like "We're Only Gonna Die" and all of the songs on *Stranger Than Fiction*, "Sorrow" grabbed me. Within a few months I had bought all the BR recordings I didn't already own, this time on CD. I listened to them constantly—while working in the yard (now I lived in Arkansas), while training for marathons in Dallas and Anchorage, while washing the dishes. I learned that BR's front man, Greg Graffin, wasn't a professor at Boston College and never had been. Rather, he was completing a Ph.D. in evolutionary biology at Cornell.

In the late summer of 2003, I decided on a whim to send Greg Graffin an e-mail.

It's probably not accurate to say that the correspondence that followed between Greg and me led to a "relationship" or "friendship," at least not in the traditional sense of those words. I don't know that anyone can really do that through e-mail. But I do think our exchanges grew into a genuine and overall friendly conversation. We're two guys of similar age, temperament, musical taste and intellectual interests who both grew up in Southern California. We're both curious about how ideas shape behavior and cultures. We both tend to be nonconformists, though we can live within "the system" so long as it doesn't step on us or tax our individuality. We both work hard, and we're proud of what we've accomplished. We're both committed to learning. At the time of this writing, we're both in our late thirties.

A major difference between us is that Greg is an atheist songwriter whose lyrics often concern themselves with religion. I'm a Christian with a deep commitment to God that somehow coexists with a skeptical disposition toward much of what I hear people say about God.

Though I have been a Christian since my early teens, I have sometimes felt more at home with atheists than with fellow believers. Two of my favorite books were written by atheists, Albert Camus and John Kekes, and another favorite was written by a very bad example of a Christian, the British novelist and travel writer Evelyn Waugh.

---

***In his best novel,* The Plague *(1947), Camus writes of a priest, Father Paneloux, who outwardly maintained an aura of serenity as disease ravaged a quarantined city. "But from the day on which he saw a child die, something seemed to change in him. And his face bore traces of the rising tension of his thoughts." One reason Camus's writing is so powerful is that he refuses to try to explain the suffering of the innocent. Instead, his response is to be morally enraged and to try and do something to stop it. I think this is the response God wants from people.***

***The books I recommend by Kekes are* Moral Wisdom and Good Lives *(1995) and* Facing Evil *(1990). Kekes's approach is stoical, less from the soul than from the disciplined mind, but he has powerful and realistic insight into the human condition. Of course, Kekes never uses the theological concept of the Fall, but his moral philosophy springs from a serious assessment of the fallen world.***

**Preston Jones**

---

I mention these writers in my letters (see pages 46-48), and I have added relevant quotes from them to this book. Evelyn Waugh's great novel *Brideshead Revisited* became a topic of discussion between Greg and me. If you haven't read this novel, or seen the BBC film production of it, I hope you will.

I suppose that sometimes I've felt more at ease with thoughtful atheists than with Christians because atheists often come to their beliefs after asking difficult questions about evil, suffering and the seeming indifference of the universe. I grew up in a very tough neighborhood; three kids I knew personally were murdered, and I myself was shot at and mobbed by thugs. A few years ago, a guy I didn't know took four bullets to the head in my parents' driveway.

Curiously, perhaps, I have never questioned God about the violence in the neighborhood I grew up in. It has always been clear to me that the people who made that neighborhood the way it was could have done otherwise. They've had access to educational opportunities, counseling and job training. They're responsible for the mess they created.

But I saw a lot during my time in the Navy (1986 to 1990) that knocked me off balance. My Sunday school lessons didn't seem to help me understand what I saw in the Philippines and Thailand, though they did help to keep me out of trouble.

As I have grown older, I've often thought that, as great and important as the churches I grew up in were, and as grateful as I am for the basic moral lessons I learned in them (which over the years helped me avoid many personal disasters), they really didn't seem to take the Bible seriously as a commentary on the complicated, crazy, amazing and often frightening human situation. It's such a ferociously realistic, truthful and profound book.

Sometimes I think that American Christians are reluctant to face the profundity of the Bible and Christian tradition. I don't think it's because they're Christians. I think it's because they're Americans. I don't mean to sound anti-American—my students can assure you I'm not. But I'm hardly the first person to recognize that the United States isn't a country that values the life of the mind. As a generalization, it seems safe to say that Americans prefer Wal-Mart to libraries, Big Macs to big ideas, and TV to education. This worries me, and I find that for whatever reason, many atheists, like Greg, share my concerns.

***In places like Olongapo [in the Philippines] something malicious had its way—not only in the brothels [where young women and girls were trapped], but in the minds of a good number of my fellow sailors who found this bizarre new world too alluring to resist. Never did the omnipotent being in whom I had been taught to believe seem so absent, so weak as he did on those city blocks. Never did [the] doctrine of the total depravity of humankind seem so true. Never was I so thankful for my good fortune as a child to have had the Bible rammed down my throat by shaky-voiced old ladies. Even as I questioned God's existence, Sunday school lessons echoed in my mind.***

**Preston Jones, "The Evil That We Do" (1997)**

As you read this book it's important to remember that Greg's and my correspondence wasn't originally meant for public consumption. We wrote because we enjoyed the give and take, and for a brief space of time we had the time to devote to what we considered a private project. A couple months into our correspondence I thought that what we had written might be useful to others. Greg agreed. As the correspondence was edited for publication, some personal or peripheral material was deleted and a few sentences were inserted in various places to add clarity to a few exchanges. But nothing substantial was added to our exchanges after the fact.

Certainly, after we decided that others might be interested in our correspondence, we could have gone back and made our notes more formal; we could have added more scholarly references; we could have carefully defined the terms we used; we could have eliminated loose ends; we could have turned the conversation into a more formal debate. But we preferred to let the conversation remain what it was. I know this might make parts of the book frustrating for readers: some questions are raised but not answered, some topics are left unresolved, and the only comprehensive theme is the conversation itself.

The approach we have taken makes for an unusual book. But we think it's worthwhile for people to see what an uncanned, unorchestrated conversation between people of very different beliefs can look like. If you find yourself thinking, "Greg should have said . . ." or "Why didn't Preston say . . . ?" or "They're both wrong!" or "He should have quoted so-and-so!" then we hope you will fill in what you think is missing. Indeed, this book will be most useful to readers who participate in the conversation—with other students or a teacher in a classroom, with a study group or in their personal studies. To encourage this, I have added material that builds on the correspondence. The study guide at the end of the book will also be useful.

To Christian readers I want to say this: I know that some of what I have written and some of the positions I take might be offensive. This concerns me because, while I want to challenge people to think—and I also like being challenged—I have no interest in being merely obnoxious or dismissive. If you think I am wrong about something, I hope you will let me know.

I also should say that I don't expect professional philosophers and theologians to be impressed with my musings. I read some philosophy, psychology and theology (I wish I had more time for all three and much more), but most of the time I'm thinking about classes I need to teach, and when I have my research hat on, I study late nineteenth- and early twentieth-century North America. I'm making this correspondence available because I hope it will promote thought and conversation. This book is intended as a starting point for people interested in putting their intellects to work.

I want to emphasize that this book does not consist of a debate. I know that, despite what I say, some readers will still construe it as such. But I never kept score between Greg and myself. I never had an impulse to see who was "winning," to see which of us was making the better points. Greg didn't either. I tried to maintain this disposition throughout the editing process.

My hope is that Greg's and my correspondence will encourage people to use the brains God gave them.

*Preston Jones*
*John Brown University*

Dear Greg:

I'm a professor at a small Christian university, so you have fans on the religious side too. Mostly I listen to your CDs when I'm out training for marathons or working in the yard. The theme song for my honors Western Civ class is "Mediocre Minds"—as in, mediocrity is what we want to resist.

I hope BR stays at it for a long time—and best wishes to you with your work at Cornell (or is that completed?).

All the best,
Preston Jones

---

Dear Professor,

I finished my Ph.D. August 14th, 2003. I have gotten many requests from religious groups to give a lecture on my dissertation. It concerns the intersection of evolutionary biology and theology and the various forms of compatibility.* I have found that evolutionary biologists debase religion to a significant degree in order to make it compatible with science. They think they are doing the religious people a service by subscribing to a form of compatibilism—that is, by maintaining that religion and evolutionary biology are compatible. In most evolutionary biologists' view, there is no conflict between evolution and reli-

*Greg's dissertation, "Evolution, Monism, Atheism and the Naturalist World-View," is available at www.polypterus.org.

***Innocents burned,***
***alive at the stake***
***Tortured and dumped***
***In nameless graves***
***Centuries wane***
***Authority died***
***Scattering seeds of ancient lies***
***Child molesters***
***And Jesuits***
***Holding secret conference***
***Underneath the pontiff's nose***
***And only God will ever know***

**Greg Graffin, "Sinister Rouge,"**
***The Empire Strikes First* (2004)**

gion on one important condition: that religion is essentially atheistic! I know it sounds crazy, but that is the result of my dissertation.

I have a song coming out on next year's Bad Religion album called "Sinister Rouge," which I feel would be a good theme song for Western Civilization.

It is a song about the Inquisition and its constant besetting of our civilization. The force of the Inquisition still rears its ugly head, even today. Interestingly, no one has written the ultimate history of the Inquisition. It is a project I would love to undertake someday. Christianity will not play a friendly role in this epic. If you are aware of a history of the Inquisition, I would greatly appreciate the reference.

Sincerely,
Greg Graffin

---

Dear Greg:

I must admit that it was a kick getting a note from a guy I've listened to, off and on, for about twenty years. Congrats on your Ph.D.! Mine is in history, much easier than science. Are you on the job market for a university position now? Maybe you'll end up close by, in Tulsa or at the University of Arkansas, Fayetteville—a hip little city. I grew up in Southern California—San Bernardino, and don't miss it at all.

I'm curious about your thesis, that religion is essentially atheistic. I'll see if I can get my paws on your dissertation—I can probably get it via interlibrary loan. As you know, the science-religion nexus is hot in the academy these days. And Cornell and UCLA are great schools. You're in good shape.

Your song "Voracious March of Godliness" made me think you had an interest in the Inquisition.

I'd guess that a psychologically compelling account of the Inquisition would be really useful. It's a topic that

***By the early 1980s, Southern California was well on its way to becoming the asphalted calamity it now is, and I remember talking with friends about the disappearing fields and orange groves as we hiked foothill trails late at night, with Rush or Led Zeppelin or Peter Gabriel (or Devo, U2 or the Christian "new wave" band Undercover) blasting from a portable cassette player.***

***Our valley, the San Bernardino one, had never been one of So Cal's hip sections. The valley of the "Valley Girl" craze (circa 1982)—which, like, permanently altered casual American speech—sprouted in the distant ravines of San Fernando. And while San Bernardino was too much of a backwater for us to be up on the lesser known fashions afoot nearer to LA—and especially in The Valley—we heard from to time about the emerging punk rock "scene."***

**Preston Jones, "Punk Rocker with a Ph.D." (2003)**

lends itself to clichés and sloganeering. The task, I guess, would be to treat all involved with charity while also being critical and truthful.

Something tells me you're a Christopher Hitchens fan. Hope the gigs in San Francisco are great.

All the best,
Preston Jones

## INQUISITIONS

Dear Preston,

I don't know who Christopher Hitchens is, and I assume from your e-mail that you indeed cannot think of a reference off the top of your head regarding the Inquisition. I noticed you mentioned your interest in hearing a charitable account of the Inquisition. I have no reason to treat such an inhumane, barbaric institution as charitable.

The fact is, no one has written the account of its atrocities in succinct form, to my knowledge. The accounts given in histories

***INQUIRY BOX***

**Greg and Preston use the word "charity" differently. It comes from the Latin word *caritas,* which means "dearness," "affection," "love" and "esteem." President Abraham Lincoln used the word in his Second Inaugural Address (delivered in August 1864, near the end of the Civil War), when he called for "charity for all"—victorious Northerners and nearly defeated Southerners alike.**

**How do Greg and Preston use this word differently, and how do these different meanings lead to misunderstanding?**

of Christianity are weak and "charitable." They expect us to believe that it had nothing to do with the intransigence of a dying religion against a backdrop of gains in general public enlightenment.

Many of the accounts were written by Christians. This is like right-wing Germans writing the definitive history of the Nazi atrocities. Christians need to be educated about the barbarism of their religion's history.

If Christianity is any better today, it is only because of its scholarship and understanding of the world, not because it can revise and forget its brutal past. I see tinges of Inquisition rhetoric throughout modern Christian writing, although I avoid anything written by Christian scholars generally. I simply am not interested in learning how modern knowledge can be reconciled with outdated theology.

Sincerely,
Greg Graffin

---

Dear Greg:

My area of specialty is late nineteenth-century North America, so I don't know what's definitive as far as Inquisition goes. (I could have a research assistant do some checking.) If the Spanish Inquisition is what you're thinking of, then Simon Whitechapel's new book *Flesh Inferno: Atrocities of Torquemada and the Spanish Inquisition* might be useful but, judging from the title, it promises to be more polemical than dispassionately historical. Also there's Susan McCarthy's *Spanish Inquisition* of a few years ago. If you're interested in the broader inquisitions that include witch trials, B. P. Levack's *The Witch-Hunt in Early Modern Europe* might be good. There are more than a dozen books available on the witch trials in colonial America. If the general topic of inquisition in Western civilization is what you're interested in, then you'd probably include the anti-Christian death squads of the French Revolution, Stalinism in the Soviet Union and elsewhere, the Alien and Sedition Acts in this country, etc.

That would probably be a lifelong project.

By "charity" I meant putting aside conclusions (to the extent possible) until the study has been completed. I mean giving the people being studied a chance to try and explain themselves from within the context of their own time and worldview. Obviously one wouldn't want to construe the Inquisition as an act of charity—though I imagine that many sixteenth century people would do that. I'm all for making judgments about things that have happened in history, but I think it's also important to remember that, if I had been there, I might have done the same thing I'm criticizing or denouncing.

Sorry to be presumptuous about Hitchens. Until a while ago, he wrote a column for *The Nation*. He did that for over 20 years. His columns and your lyrics have some things in common.

Hope the gig in San Francisco went well.

All the best,
Preston

***At a provincial meeting there was an ovation when Stalin's name was mentioned, and no one dared to be the first to sit down. When, finally, an old man who could stand no longer took his seat, his name was noted and he was arrested the next day.***

**Robert Conquest, historian and political writer (1991)**

***I saw that I should keep ever before me the truth that all have sinned, and that because I am a part of the human community of sinners I can't presume myself to be superior to others—either those now living or those who have gone before. I also saw that, my own combative temperament notwithstanding, I am obliged to practice charity toward all men and women, the living and the dead.***

**Preston Jones, "History, Discernment and the Christian Life" (2001)**

***I was sitting in a bible-study class at the age of about ten . . . when the teacher began to hymn the work of God in Nature. How wonderful it was, she said, that trees and vegetation were green; the most restful color to our eyes. Imagine if instead the woods and grasses were purple, or orange. I knew nothing about chlorophyll and phototropism at that age, still less about the Argument from Design or the debate on Creationism versus Evolution. I merely remember thinking, with my childish and unformed cortex: Oh, don't be silly.***

**Christopher Hitchens, journalist and writer (2001)**

Dear Preston,

Thank you for those references and for pointing me toward Christopher Hitchens. You have touched on something I have noticed in the literature. The Spanish Inquisition seems to have much more coverage than the papal inquisition into heresy that predates the Spanish Inquisition. I think this is a case of the Spaniards' getting s*** on by scholars and receiving blame for something started by the papacy. As you probably know, there was torment throughout Europe before the Spaniards decided to bring on the Inquisition. During the early-modern witch-hunts 60,000 people were executed! I think it is high time that figures like these came to light.

Cornell University (where I did my dissertation work) has one of the best collections of medieval books and pamphlets in the country. A. D. White, the university's first president, was an avid collector and made numerous trips to Europe in the 1880s and 1890s collecting manuscripts. Among the Cornell collections are numerous testimonials of inquisitors and original works detailing case studies of heretics and methods. My advisor, Will Provine (also a historian), has assured me that to study them would require a high level of scholarship, for they are written in Old German and French and other European languages.

I have no doubt that a large-scale study of the Inquisition would be a very important contribution. But I agree with you that it is probably a lifelong goal rather than a feasible project to begin at this stage of my life.

What you are calling "charity" is a normal matter of course for us naturalists. We do not form conclusions until the data is analyzed. However, it takes little data to conclude that those who were tortured in the name of the church were done wrong by the church and I can't see any reason to defend the church (I find even less reason to defend the Catholic church in its pathetic downward spiral in modern society, given the rash of child molestation cases coming to light). Rather, I find it necessary to enlighten people about a better way. That way is naturalism.

The intolerance of the Inquisition is, I believe, a natural outcome of traditional theology. History is the result of causes. Although we probably can't always figure out exactly what caused certain things to happen in history, we can examine some of the dominating factors. I believe the Inquisition, which was part of a culture of fear and intolerance justified by theology, was one such factor that still rears its ugly head in our world. That is one reason

I don't believe Christianity has much to offer.

I think it is inaccurate to portray anti-Christian death squads as part of the Inquisition. I believe any kind of death squad is wrong. But let's not confuse radical splinter groups with cultural norms based on Christian intolerance. The Inquisition was the latter, the death squads are the former.

Well, this has gone on too long and I have a show in an hour. I appreciate your interest and it is fun to chat with a historian who is also a defender of Christianity.

Sincerely,
Greg Graffin

*Preston does not immediately respond to Greg's point about Christianity and violence here, but returns to this theme on pages 134-39. Also see the study guide at the back of the book.*

---

Dear Greg:

Wish I could have been at the show in San Francisco, or at any of the shows. The last concert I saw in S.F. was the Cocteau Twins in 1997, just before they split up.

It's tough to imagine bands as different as the Twins and BR, but they're both among my favorites. Opposites attract?

It's like that with people too. Some of the folks who've had the greatest influence on me have been devout Christians (mostly Catholics and Anglicans); some of the others have been atheists—e.g., John Kekes, a moral philosopher at SUNY Albany; Christopher Hitchens, the rabid, self-proclaimed "anti-theist" journalist; and Albert Camus.

Mediocrities of any stripe don't do the world any good. If you're going to follow Jesus, then you'll have to pass up the mealy-mouth stuff dished out at most churches; if you're gonna hate God, then do it right (he can take care of himself).

---

***It's as difficult to describe the Cocteau Twins' music as it is to understand the "lyrics" of the band's singer, Liz Fraser. For their later recordings, perhaps "ethereal" is a good word. The recording* Stars and Topsoil *(2000) provides a good overview of the band's career, though the record* Blue Bell Knoll *(1995) is probably the best place for the uninitiated to start.***

**Preston Jones**

---

I'm not sure what to do with the perverted, rapist priests. Loathe, pity, punish and forgive all at once? I confess that it is hard to believe that the Catholic church has any special connection to God, given all the nonsense and brutality that's taken place within it over the years. That's one reason I haven't actually become Catholic. But there's power in the liturgy and the Mass. Actually, I'm an Anglican. But the Episcopal church in this country is a disaster. The local Catholic church is the closest thing to Anglicanism I can find.

Your note made me think about a lot of things, and if my gorgeous baby girl weren't crying right now I'd fill you in. For now, let me say that you're right to imply that there is something barbaric at the heart of Christianity. God wanted blood, first of animals, then of his son.

I started Latin at 32 and Greek at 34. (I'm 36 now.) So there's time for you to learn the languages you need and to write a definitive history.

Peace,
Preston

---

Dear Preston,

I am impressed by your breadth of inspirational intellectuals and by your learning of Latin and Greek. Did you take classes? Or learn "Berlitz"? I guess I had better start learning; I'm 38.

I agree with you that it is nearly impossible to summarize what I think about the child-molesting priests in a couple of sentences. It requires a long explanation.

Is the anti-theist Hitchens a naturalist? What is his academic background?

Sincerely,
Greg

## HATING GOD

Dear Greg:

Hitchens graduated from an English boarding school and Oxford, but he never went to graduate school—or at least he never got a graduate degree. He was probably too smart for that. On the strength of his fierce and sometimes devastating polemical writing, he teaches occasional classes at Stanford, Berkeley, City College and other places. I think he's actually a professor somewhere now. I'm not sure if he's an atheist or an outright God-hater—maybe both, though it's hard to see why one would spend one's time hating something that doesn't exist. (Maybe the hatred for God atheists feel is a proof of God's existence.) He quit *The Nation* and now writes reviews for *The Atlantic*, and he has long written for *Vanity Fair*. I've seen him refer to himself at different times as a Marxist and a libertarian—I'm not quite sure how that works!

First I learned French (while I was in the Navy). That was a bridge to Latin—I took a class at a junior college in northern California when I taught in the California State University system. Once you get a feel for Latin grammar, Greek is a little easier. I sat in on a Greek class at a prep school I taught at in Texas, and am sitting in on another one at the university now. I've also studied Welsh for about 12 years. It's a ridiculously difficult language. I also dabble in Anglo-Saxon (Old English).

What's your dissertation title? I tried to find it on the Internet but only found tributes to you from your international fan club.

Have fun at the gig in Denver.

Peace,
Preston

---

Dear Preston,

My dissertation probably hasn't been microfilmed yet. If you want to wait, I can send you a copy when I get home in a couple weeks. The title is "Monism, Atheism, and the Naturalist World-View: Perspectives from Evolutionary Biology."

***I sat on my bed and said to God . . . You haven't got me yet. I know Your cunning. It's You who take us up to a high place and offer us the whole universe. You're a devil, God, tempting us to leap. But I don't want Your peace and I don't want Your love. . . . With Your great schemes You ruin our happiness as a harvester ruins a mouse's nest. I hate You, God, I hate You as though You existed.***

**Graham Greene, novelist, *The End of the Affair***

Although it is a chuckle to read your idea that hating God might be evidence of God's existence, it is misleading to believe that such a behavior could imply God's existence. Science requires more than that, as I am sure you are aware. It would be a great trick by God, however.

I cannot understand the concept of hating God.

I neither love nor hate the universe, so it seems odd that some people rail so heavily against the inevitable. What is difficult for me—and I find myself intolerant at times—is that people can so blindly believe in God. For the average citizen, it is because of their fear and lack of reasoning capacity or desire. For the educated, it is from a lack of scientific education. The more I talk to educated people the more I verify my belief.

God is an answer for people who have no idea how the physical world works. Now, if you combine knowledge of how the world works with fear induced through theological "education" during youth, you have religious scientists who can accurately identify the gaps in scientific knowledge and are compelled to fill them with God's wisdom or plan or whatever. That pisses me off.

But by and large, if someone says he is an atheist, or a theist for that matter, I don't really take the person very seriously unless he can demonstrate a fair knowledge of natural phenomena.

Sincerely,
Greg Graffin

## ODD CHRISTIANS AND NATURALISM

Dear Greg:

I would like to get my hands on your dissertation. It sounds interesting. I liked your line that an atheist's irrational hatred of God being a "proof" for God's existence would be a great trick by God. You probably wrote that in a spirit of irony, but there's reason to think that God does that sort of thing, arranging life in such a way that people eventually get to enjoy the joke too, though sometimes the joke isn't so funny.

I've mentioned before some of the atheists who've had a big influence on me. Among the Christians who've influenced me the most are a tobacco-chewing janitor who saw visions of the Virgin Mary and a schizophrenic who lived in a mental hospital I worked at for a year. Jesus' family tree includes a murderer and a whore, and the Bible's full of nutcases (Samson, Jonah, John the Baptist).

Paul snuffed a bunch of Christians before he became one. Billy Graham is simple, but charitable organizations he's associated with have fed millions and he's done a lot of good.

Before you bend the knee again before the altar of "naturalism" (I never took you for a dogmatist), I want to ask what the vision of the world your lyrics frequently

***The word of the LORD came to Jonah son of Amittai: "Go to the great city of Nineveh and preach against it." . . . But Jonah ran away from the LORD. . . . He went down to Joppa, where he found a ship bound for [Tarshish]. . . . Then the LORD sent a great wind on the sea, and such a violent storm arose that the ship threatened to break up. . . . [The crew] asked him, "What should we do . . . to make the sea calm down for us?"***

***"Pick me up and throw me into the sea," he replied. . . . The LORD provided a great fish to swallow Jonah. . . . From inside the fish Jonah prayed to the LORD his God. . . . Jonah obeyed the word of the LORD and went to Nineveh.***

**Jonah 1:1—3:3**

express has to do with an impersonal universe that is the way it is because it can't be any other way—just because that's the way it is. If the universe is the way it is just because that's the way it is, and we are part of the universe, then what's all this stuff about the world being better "when soldiers lay their weapons down; when all kings and queens . . . relinquish their crowns," etc.? I'm cynical, but not so cynical as to think that you meant this as a parody or satire of people who think that the world can be made better. I really think you hope the world (or some as-

***A record of the genealogy of Jesus Christ: . . . Rahab . . . King David.***

**Matthew 1:1-6**

pects of the human part of the world) can be made better. I hope for the same thing.

But how can it make sense for people who are part of this "inevitable," impersonal, just-as-it's-supposed-to-be universe to want to change part of it, i.e., the behavior of others who are also part of the same universe? If we are really just a part of this impersonal universe and no more, then how would we know that something is wrong with the universe we're part and parcel of? Humans have within them (from some source) a sense that things can be better. But this couldn't come from the stuff of a just-as-it's-supposed-to-be universe. It has to come from somewhere else.

A utilitarian answer won't suffice—e.g., humans want a better life for others because they've figured out that that means a better life for themselves. That might explain why I pick up the trash my neighbor lets collect in front of his house. It doesn't explain why I spend some of my free time agitating against the U.S. military's ongoing support for the Southeast Asian sex trade. Whether the kiddie slaves in the brothels of Bangkok are liberated or not has no direct bearing on my day-to-day life. I'm enraged by their plight out of a sense that a great injustice is being perpetrated. And I don't see how such a sense of rage could spring from the stuff of a just-as-it's-supposed-to-be universe.

***I think naturalism fails at very interesting points. I don't think naturalism informs me at all about why I leave a tip in a restaurant in the middle of England when I'll never be there again in my life.***

**Henry Harpending, geneticist (2003)**

I know a little about neuropsychology, behaviorism, etc. But certain human essences remained uncaptured.

Best,
Preston

---

Dear Preston,

I think you have been given a very strange and biased view of naturalism. Much of the characterizing you do of naturalism is not accurate. The naturalism I, and most scientists I have interviewed and learned from, subscribe to is simply the belief that truth comes from the empirical investigation of the universe.

By "morality" I am referring to the social rules we are all familiar with—for example, if you borrow something give it back, and help the disabled. It has no necessary connection with religion, or any other institution for that matter. It is the behavior we learn from our earliest development, from our immediate social encounters (usually this is parents and siblings).

Making the world a better place is a major goal for me. But do not mistake my intentions to educate people to live better with the belief that our ultimate destiny is changeable. We are indeed headed for extinction just as sure as we will die in a short time as individuals. This depresses a lot of people. I accept it as I accept taxes. No use ruining a good meal over undue worry about the tariffs applied to the wine. Life can be better, socially and morally.

***We need a fresh and new religion to run our lives.***

**Greg Graffin, "Kyoto Now!" *The Process of Belief* (2002)**

Naturalism presents a way to understand the world, to under-

***Proximate meaning:* A sense of meaning or purpose derived from action in the observable world.**

***Ultimate meaning:* A sense of meaning or purpose derived from belief, and from acting on belief, in a reality beyond or greater than the observable world.**

**Preston Jones**

stand people better, to learn why things are the way they are, how they came to be. These are the most satisfying aspects of human brain function. Traditional religion offers nothing satisfying now because science explains such things better. In fact, all that is left for religion is to claim authority over issues of morality. Yuck!

***I have never found a question answered better by God than . . . by science. I guess, in that respect, science has become a religion to me, but only because it is based on testable hypotheses.***

**Greg Graffin, interview in *HM* magazine (1993)**

Morality need not be connected with any institution. It is a part of human development. If traditional religion were necessary for morality, I would be considered amoral, and that's an outright offense to me and my children, and anyone who considers me a good citizen.

Naturalism is a young, new religion. It is satisfying because it is a teacher. It is not purposeless; it merely focuses on proximate meaning instead of ultimate meaning. Ultimate meaning is what traditional religion clings to, desperately trying to remain relevant.

Religion is only relevant because it is drilled into so many children's heads as being important (they grow up and believe what they learned as kids). A society raised without traditional theology is just as moral, just as charitable, and probably more worldly and open to a variety of opinion than ours is currently.

I have never concerned myself with ultimate meaning, but I have a deeply meaningful life. I am privileged to have a deep effect on the way lots of people think—most importantly for me, my two children. I have a wonderful circle of friends and a loving interpersonal relationship with my girlfriend. I was never baptized, never aware of a single story from the Good Book, never programmed by religious teachers, and never concerned about life after death. Rather, naturalism teaches one of the most important things in this world: there is only this life, so live wonderfully and meaningfully.

A great beginning, if you are interested in a better education about naturalism, is Homer Smith's *Man and His Gods*. Also, I highly recommend Julian Huxley's *Religion Without Revelation*. Anything by E. O. Wilson is also great.

Many people have found ways to find meaning in the world without subscribing to the notion of ultimate meaning, a concept traditional religion is obsessed with but one that renders traditional religion as intellectually stagnant and militantly authoritarian as ever.

I am dogmatic about one thing: learning is a lifelong pursuit. Anything that stands in the way of free learning, discovery and verification is harmful to mankind. Theology has a history of such a malevolent tradition. Natural science does not. I choose science to educate me and rely on the great work of my parents to become a good person.

Sincerely,
Greg

***Man's most sacred duty, and at the same time his most glorious opportunity, is to promote the maximum fulfillment of the evolutionary process on earth.***

**Julian Huxley, biologist and author (1957)**

***The choice between transcendentalism and empiricism will be the coming century's vision of the struggle for men's souls. Moral reasoning will either remain centered in the idioms of theology and philosophy . . . or it will shift toward science-based material analysis.***

**E. O. Wilson, biologist (1998)**

***History . . . reveals that man does not need any brand of transcendental metaphysics—his lasting contentments and achievements he has found wholly within the frame of reference that takes things as they are in the here and now.***

**Homer W. Smith, physiologist (1952)**

## THE TOUGH WORLD

Dear Greg:

I've just returned from the racquetball court, where I got my butt kicked in three consecutive games by a guy in his mid-fifties who's up for major surgery in a few weeks—and I run marathons! That's a reality check.

I appreciate your note. There's a lot to respond to. The only thing I'll say now is that you're obviously right that "truth comes from the empirical investigation of the universe." But who, really, believes that the sum of all truth lies there?

The feelings you have for your children (and that I have for my daughter) are inextricably linked to physical-neurological activity and psychological processes. Snip off the relevant piece of my brain (so to speak), and I would lose the capacity to feel love for my daughter. Yet I can't imagine a neuropsychologist, who isn't himself a humanoid, saying that a father's love for his child is only the sum of these processes.

***In the case of living systems, nobody would deny that an organism [such as person] is a collection of atoms. The mistake is to suppose that it is nothing but a collection of atoms. Such a claim is as ridiculous as asserting that a Beethoven symphony is nothing but a collection of notes or that a Dickens novel is nothing but a collection of words.***

**Paul Davies, physicist (1983)**

One studies all of the processes, reads all the available literature, appreciates the wondrous complexity of the human psyche without reference to a potential metaphysical designer, and one still has to say that there is something fundamentally ineffable, something inexplicably blessed, something unfathomably deep about the feelings you have for your children—about the feeling I felt a moment ago when my 17-month-old daughter came into the office to say hello. Of course, empiricism is the way to go. But even given all its staggering achievements and potential, it's limited in what it can do. It seems that to hold only to that is to tie oneself to an article of faith more limited than any narrow theological fundamentalism.

And I want to hold to my claim that naturalism as a complete outlook on life is self-defeating. It seems to say that the universe is indifferent, and we are part of the universe, yet we are not indifferent. The universe knows nothing about love, and we are part of the universe, yet we love and seek to be loved. The universe doesn't care if we live or die, we are part of the universe, yet we would rather live through tomorrow than die tomorrow. Sure, all these human sentiments can be taken to pieces in a lab, labeled, and written up in the journals. But why humans should behave in a way so at odds with the universe they live in would, I suspect, remain a mystery.

But I also noted how much we agree in terms of general outlook—which doesn't surprise me. Like you, I know that even if I am successful at making a small part of the world better, the general trend is in the direction of oblivion. People are self-destructive—I think of overfed Americans watching three hours of TV a day; of corrupt African governments starving their people, who then slaughter one another in ethnic and tribal conflict; of mindless reproduction in spite of poverty; of poor use of water, etc. And I know that if we don't kill ourselves off, or if some power greater than us doesn't intervene, then eventually the sun will burn out.

This may sound strange coming from a Christian, but I would also prefer that there weren't an afterlife. But I know that an empirical study would show that the overwhelming majority of people who have lived and who live now, regardless of religious affiliation, have a sense that there is something to come after this life. Most of the time since I've been a Christian (since 1981) I have been generally indifferent to the concept of heaven. I'm not sure that's a good thing, though, and I know a lot of Christians would wonder if a person who doesn't care about the possibility of heaven really could be a Christian. I guess my explanation is that I owe everything worthwhile in my life to Christianity, and that's good enough.

Now Bad Religion is back in the asphalted jungle that is Southern California. Have a great time at the gigs. Tell the punkers in the crowd I said hello!

Best,
Preston

---

Dear Preston,

I am curious about the following that you wrote: "The only thing I'll say now is that you're obviously right that 'truth comes from the empirical investigation of the universe.' But who, really, believes that the sum of all truth lies there?" I will answer that question: I do. The only people who don't believe that truth lies there are philosophers and theologians who have for centuries insisted that the sum of all truth lies somewhere "ineffable" or somewhere beyond. That is a pernicious myth that has only very recently begun to be exposed as detrimental.

I am convinced that, in time, as we abolish the myth that truth is something larger than our naturalistic investigations, fewer and fewer people will find it necessary to subscribe to the supernatural.

There is no sense of loss in acknowledging that what we discover is all that exists. It does not imply that we have discovered everything in the universe—in fact it would be an error of judgment (played out often in the history of Western civilization) to assume all is known already. But in advocating that we now have a method for discovering the truth—naturalism—we can be filled with a sense of hope for the future of our society and our children. This is an excellent replacement for the hopeless theological suggestion that an unknown but somehow better life awaits us after we die.

***If all the achievements of scientists were wiped out tomorrow, there would be no doctors but witch doctors, no transport faster than horses, no computers, no printed books, no agriculture beyond subsistence peasant farming. If all the achievements of theologians were wiped out tomorrow, would anyone notice the smallest difference?***

**Richard Dawkins, evolutionary biologist (1998)**

Now, no amount of science or naturalistic explanation can substitute for the human emotion that I feel for my children or interpersonal relations. But that is not truth in any important measure of the word. That is hardly even knowledge. Those are feelings and feelings aren't truth. Truth and knowledge are social phenomena. They are a part of the collective activity of human social groups.

The religious "truth" that affects the social groups who think of themselves as religious is not useful for human society.

In fact, more conflict has arisen over religious "truth" historically than any other factor. Real truth, the kind discovered by naturalists, is useful for all mankind, and all social groups. It is not a replacement for feelings, but feelings are totally individualistic, perceived and interpreted differently by each human being.

Interpersonally, and perhaps even socially to some degree, it

> ***You create your own reality***
>
> ***And leave mine to me.***
>
> **Greg Graffin, "Leave Mine to Me,"** ***Stranger Than Fiction*** **(1994)**

is crucial to maintain some form of agreement about what good feelings and bad feelings are—that is the essence of morals, which are not necessarily prescribed by religions. Those social agreements are often unwritten because of the similar emotional systems that have evolved in our species.

I think humans have a general predisposition to form similar ideas of what a good feeling is and what a bad feeling is. That is why so many religions have similar "commandments," even though they were developed totally independently in time and geography. Religious types might say that is evidence for God. Naturalists say it is evidence for no God.

In any event, if people want to believe in God, I have no problem with them. But if they want to tell me that God is a kind of truth or knowledge that I am ignorant of, I ask them how I can be more educated. They usually say, "First you have to have faith." Then I realize their knowledge is something that is personal and holds nothing for me, or for society. I have written many songs about this, in fact.

Sincerely,
Greg

## BOOKS

Dear Greg:

I appreciate the time you take to write; I know you're busy. Of course, I'm busy too—but I look forward to hearing from you. I spend my days with Christians, many of whom are very bright, a few of whom are brilliant. But it is nice to get out of that neighborhood, so to speak.

***The world of today needs Christians who remain Christians. . . . What the world expects of Christians is that Christians should speak out, loud and clear, and they should voice their condemnation [of evil] in such a way that never a doubt, never the slightest doubt, could rise in the heart of the simplest man.***

**Albert Camus, philosopher and writer (1948)**

I'm going to take up your suggestion and read Homer Smith's book and something by E. O. Wilson. Would you recommend *Consilience?*

At the end of my high school years I read a lot of stuff by atheists—Camus, Sartre, the Huxleys and Bertrand Russell. In the end I was deeply impressed only with Camus. In addition to his deep humanity, I appreciated that he had taken the time to study serious Christian philosophy—much of his dissertation concerned the thought of St. Augustine, and he knew that the Bible was serious literature.

My surmise (shared by some scholars) is that he had become a Christian, albeit a very idiosyncratic one, before his death, or that he was very close to doing so. Even if I didn't think that, I'd still value his writing immensely. He saw deeply into simple things.

Bertrand Russell's general essays struck me as fatuous garbage, and I've never felt compelled to change that view. I did ostentatiously read his book *Why I Am Not a Christian* at a Billy Graham "crusade" in Anaheim, but that's the only fun I gained from his flimsy polemics. (His *History of Western Philosophy*, on the other hand, is good.)

I honestly don't remember much about the Huxleys, except that I was reading Aldous's book *The Doors of Perception* on the value of hallucinogenic drugs when I was in the Navy, and an officer who happened to see me didn't approve. (Not that I had any interest in taking drugs at the time. I was just on a Huxley kick.)

***INQUIRY BOX***

**This is one of the sentences in Russell's *Why I Am Not a Christian* that I underlined at the Graham crusade:**

> **The knowledge exists by which universal happiness can be secured; the chief obstacle to its utilization for that purpose is the teaching of religion.**

**This sentence was published in 1930, before the major anti-Christian ideologies of Nazism and Communism (in Stalin's Soviet Union) let loose unprecedented terror. But even now that Nazism and Stalinist Communism have been defeated, "universal happiness" seems a long way off.**

**Do you think universal happiness is achievable? Does secularism make it more achievable? What does it say about people that they desire universal happiness but have never experienced it? Where does this desire come from?**

More than any other contemporary scholar, John Kekes at SUNY Albany has had a deep influence on me. His books *Moral Wisdom and Good Lives* and *Facing Evil* are, I think, excellent. They have changed how I see everyday life. It's strange that in my mind this atheist sees more deeply into the consequences of what Christians call "the Fall" than any theologian I've read. Like Camus, he sees deeply into ordinary things.

If I could convince you to read something, I would say that you should read the four Gospels in the New Testament and Evelyn Waugh's novel *Brideshead Revisited.*

Here's my rationale for the Gospels: I gather from an earlier note that you're not very familiar with the Bible. That's common these days. But simply as an educational matter, a general knowledge of the Bible is crucial to understanding much of Western history (and, increasingly, global history). Also, our literature is full of biblical allusions. And the God Western atheists don't believe in is, so to speak, the biblical one. The Bible is basic literature with which, I think, all educated people in Western societies should be at least passingly familiar.

***Human motives are mixed and . . . we are complex beings. We are moved by the good, but we are also moved by evil. Our virtues coexist and conflict with our vices. The inner life of the overwhelming majority of us is a struggle in which confused motives, lack of self-knowledge, defective judgment, inflated sense of self-importance, fantasy, greed, as well as love, decency, pity, and a sense of justice are the soldiers of the ignorant armies clashing in the dark.***

**John Kekes, moral philosopher (1995)**

And I recommend Waugh's novel, partly because it's one of my favorites (there's a nine-hour BBC production of the novel that is amazingly good), and partly because in some ways you remind me of its main character, Charles Ryder.

Don't forget to tell the crowd in tonight's West Hollywood audience that I said hello—especially the drunkards!

Peace,
Preston

---

Dear Preston,

There are no drunkards at our shows, only intellectuals! Well, if that were true our show tonight would probably be pretty boring. There is room for all at a Bad Religion concert.

Thanks for the tip on reading the Gospels. I am usually put off by contradictory texts, and from what I have read by non-Christian scholars, there is a fair degree of contradiction in the Gospels. But I appreciate what you say about their importance and perhaps I will read them soon.

Did you know that my great-grandfather, E. M. Zerr, wrote a multi-volume Bible commentary in the 1930s that is still in use in rural areas of the Midwest in a sect called Church of Christ?

Could I just watch the BBC version instead of reading the *Brideshead* novel? I know my dad, an English professor, would be ashamed of me for asking that, but if it's a good adaptation, I don't mind watching the novel!

Catch you later.

Sincerely,
Greg

Dear Greg:

My head is pounding with a flu passed on to me from the dear little one.

I think some of my students were pretty weirded out the other day when I played "Mediocre Minds" in class. I handed out the lyrics beforehand. There are a couple BR fans in the class.

Each year my wife and I have a "Brideshead Weekend," when we watch the nine-hour series. It follows the book nearly verbatim. It's the nearest thing to cinematic literature I've seen. I didn't really "get" the book till I saw the BBC series, so I think your idea's a good one.

---

***Where all are Christians, the situation is this: to call oneself a Christian is the means whereby one secures oneself against all sorts of inconveniences and discomforts, and the means whereby one secures worldly goods, comforts, profit, etc., etc. But we make as if nothing had happened, we declaim about believing, . . . about confessing Christ before the world, about following him, etc., etc.; and orthodoxy flourishes in the land . . . orthodoxy everywhere, the orthodoxy which consists in playing the game of Christianity.***

**Søren Kierkegaard, philosopher (1855)**

---

There's a Church of Christ just around the corner from my house. I don't know much about that denomination, though I've heard that members of some of its subgroups hold beliefs that aren't held by Protestants generally. I looked up one of your great-grandfather's commentaries. He wrote in 1958 that "public confession is necessary for salvation." So, in other words, people can't go to heaven unless they publicly confess their faith in Christ. That must sound nuts to you since, in your view, the whole argument is based on bogus premises. I know what he means, but one can think of a lot of exceptions that would throw the rule in doubt—e.g., the person in a car accident who dies before anyone arrives, the person living in a dictatorship who concludes that working quietly as a Christian is more likely to produce good results than to go public, and so on.

Most liberal denominations are similar these days in that they offer a wimpy Christianized form of political correctness. Generally speaking, most conservative denominations don't harp as much on their denominational distinctiveness as they used to. In fact, one of the benefits of the prevailing secularism is that it has forced Christians to give up petty disputes. I really think that Christianity will be much better off when, as in the first few centuries after its founding, the people who claim to adhere to it are cultural outsiders.

Jesus, Paul, Peter and the rest were hardly political insiders.

I think I mentioned before that I'm a Protestant who attends a Catholic church. The Catholic Church is probably the most ridiculous and the most profound institution in the world.

Say hello to the intellectuals in the mosh pit for me.

Peace,
Preston

Dear Preston,

Just for your information: I am flattered that you would use a song of mine to play for your students. However, "Mediocre Minds" was a very coarsely thrown-together song, one that I spent very little time composing. It is not one of my favorites and I'm actually a bit shy about admitting I wrote it. (Mr. Hetson wrote the music.) That is about the only song in our catalog that I shy away from, believe it or not. But I am glad it means something to you nonetheless.

I am in the middle of a week of shows, seven in a row! This is unheard of at my age. I usually do three then a day off, three more, then a day off, etc. I haven't done seven in a row for fifteen years. I am getting through it.

Sincerely,
Greg

## THEISM VERSUS NATURALISM

*The dialogue that follows consists of an e-mail Preston wrote to Greg, to which Greg responded point by point within the text of Preston's original message. This format has been retained, with the addition of some textual cues (differrent fonts) and the writers' initials) to help guide readers.*

Dear Greg:

I want to pass some thoughts by you on why naturalism would be a very weak replacement for Christian theism (I can't speak for any other religious outlook). I know you're busy, so I'll try to keep it brief. . . .

Dear Preston,

Your e-mail has so many statements that are muddled! I hope you will see why your suppositions are so hard to interpret. They are one-sided at best, and hopefully you will realize that there is a better way to look at these issues, and a more correct way to express the philosophical problems. . . .

PJ: One thing that comes to mind is that theism has the advantage of being able to absorb the findings of "naturalistic investigations" while naturalism can, at best, hope only to capture some of the ground held by theism.

GG: This is a very practical problem, but not a very serious one in the grand scheme. Who cares if a body of knowledge is not accommodating? I thought we were interested in whether it is better at explaining the natural world. Theists have a difficult time explaining natural phenomena in any reasonable way consistent with the facts of nature. Humans are a part of nature; theists have a hard time explaining human nature to scientists who know better.

PJ: Here's what I mean: I'm told that a new subfield called "neurotheology" is now coming into being. This field involves studying how people seem to be "wired" for religion—and the basic findings suggest that, yes, at least some people seem to be neurologically (or otherwise) prone to be religious. Another social scientific finding is that some personality types are more attracted to religious commitment and thought than others. A third is that people, and especially men, tend to think about God the way they think about their fathers.

The theist should have no problem accepting these findings. In the first case, it makes sense that a being who, in one way or another, brought humans into existence would wire them in such a way that they would be interested in him (the being). In the second case, the New Testament observes that, for whatever reason, God gives some people a larger "measure of faith" than he gives to others. This finding about personalities and faith seems to support that claim.

***Do not think of yourself more highly than you ought, but rather think of yourself with sober judgment, in accordance with the measure of faith God has given you.***

**St. Paul, Letter to the Romans 12:3**

In the third case, the New Testament encourages fathers to honor their children (a point of view that I think is fairly unique in ancient literature). This psychological finding that children tend to think about God as they think about their fathers might give us some insight into why the N.T. does that. In other words, the theist can accept all these naturalistic findings and walk away, not with his worldview challenged, but strengthened.

What would the naturalist who is unwilling to entertain the possibility of metaphysics do with these findings?

GG: I am a scientist. I am deeply interested in metaphysics. You have made a grave error in judgment assuming that biologists are not interested in metaphysics. In fact, it is upon the topic of metaphysics that the entire conflict between evolution and religion hinges. Metaphysics is concerned with the question, "what exists?"

My null hypothesis, like most atheists', is that no gods exist. If something exists, then a naturalist believes she can find evidence of it. If no evidence is found, we have to conclude that it either doesn't exist—i.e., the possibility of its existence is nullified—or we haven't figured out a way to discover it yet. But it is foolish to assume that just because we haven't figured out a way to discover something, it will remain forever beyond the scope of naturalism.

I interviewed the Oxford evolutionary biologist Richard Dawkins about this very topic and he put it this way: Things "out there" that haven't been discovered yet are "waiting to be drawn into the embrace of naturalism." Now, some religious people say, "God is waiting to be discovered and I have faith that he is out there." I am willing to allow for such blind faith, but I offer this: Whatever god is waiting out there, it's nothing like the traditional gods of our religions and it seems to be continually eluding us and shows every manifestation of not caring about us or our plant and animal relatives. If one wants to call God nature, I have no problem with that either. (I prefer to call it nature, not God, but I try to avoid the term usually.) But, again, that is nothing like the theistic God Americans seem to hold so dear. So you see, metaphysics is not only an interesting topic to most scientists, it is essential to naturalism.

PJ: I suppose the naturalist might say something like, "See, religion has only to do with neurochemical and psychological processes. It's materialistic from beginning to end."

GG: This is exactly what a naturalist would say. And the fact that religion is created in the minds of human beings suggests that God is created in the minds of human beings, and God itself (or whatever) does not exist. There is no metaphysical reality to God. God is an epiphenomenon of the human brain.

Why do so many humans have the tendency to believe in God? Well, again, the interviews I did as part of my doctoral work shed light on this. There might be a genetic predisposition in the developing child's brain to believe what parents say. This is very reasonable since the earliest social interactions we have are with our parents or immediate familial social group. The stories and "truths" we are told in the first six or seven years of life are what form our worldview. Pervasive stories in our society perpetuate and change very, very slowly. (Remember it took about 300 years for the general population to believe the stories elucidated by Copernicus that the sun, not the earth, is the center of the solar system!) Evolution still hasn't caught on universally, particularly in the USA where children are taught ancient creation stories instead of modern evolution stories. I predict it will be another 100 years, if education isn't totally corrupted, before Americans understand and accept Darwinism.

In any event, children grow up and become university professors and join psychology departments. Then they write books with theses like "god exists in our neurons" or some other nonsense, completely muddling the issue of metaphysics.

In short, if God is no more than neurons in action, God doesn't exist! It is the burden of the theist to demonstrate that God exists outside the neurons.

Attempting to show that the universe is elaborately designed doesn't discount evolution to any degree and it certainly doesn't suggest to me that there is a God. It just means some very elaborate things can materialize given enough time. (This is something most theists fail to appreciate: try counting up to one million. If you did this as a full-time job, it would take you a year and a half of work. Multicellular life has existed for over 500 million years! The time scale is mind-boggling, but calculable.)

PJ: Then you pose the question to the naturalist: "Why do people sense that life has meaning beyond itself? Why are people kind to strangers they will never meet again? Why have the overwhelming majority of people through time believed in intelligent spiritual agents?" And it seems that the naturalist would be forced to say that, while these phenomena may be socially useful in some ways, they are fundamentally absurd because what they seem to suggest to people about reality is false or misleading.

GG: I can't overstate how inaccurate and unsatisfying an answer this would be. No thoughtful naturalist would ever say such a thing. Here's one reason why, off the top of my head: love toward another person (children excepted from this example) is a feeling, an emotion, a drive toward something that is very difficult to put into words. There is nothing but faith when one agrees to a loving relationship with another person. When a love dissolves and the relationship ends, is it prudent to say, "Wow, that was meaningless, pointless, and love therefore has no meaning?" No; in fact, in my experience, I have learned a lot from past relationships, and I have gone on to love other people. There is a drive in my mind toward loving. This is because I am a social organism and whatever physicochemical causes are present to create my love drive have served my ancestors well in forming a social species. It is a part of being human to have these drives and it unifies us as a social group.

PJ: Which brings us back to the fundamental problem with raw naturalism: It can't explain why people long for ultimate meaning when they live in a world that comprises only proximate and relative meaning.

GG: I just explained how the drive for meaning can be a physicochemical process. The focus on ultimate meaning is a story told to us as we develop that ultimate meaning is more important than proximate meaning. I think you have a hard task ahead of you if you want to assert that ultimate meaning is what the mind focuses on. You can ask a million people and they all might say, "Yes, I focus entirely on ultimate meaning," but perhaps as many as 99 percent of them have been told a story as a developing child about the ultimate story of God. The only meaningful study would be to find a group of people who were raised in a culture of proximate meaning stories and see if they longed for an ultimate explanation. My hypothesis is that they would not. I feel fine not having any need for ultimate explanations. It might be the key to my happiness, in fact!

PJ: A world made only of soft things couldn't produce a concept of hardness. A world made only of blue things couldn't produce a concept of red. A world that is ultimately meaningless couldn't produce a concept of ultimate meaning.

GG: With all due respect, my friend, this sounds like philosophical nonsense. Philosophers love to sit around and talk about this stuff, which very few naturalists take seriously. It is not very hip with current neurobiology.

PJ: It's true that theism can't explain why this is true in a way that would satisfy a person looking for leak-proof answers. But the answers it can provide seem more plausible than those raw naturalists can provide, partly because theists are in a position to add to naturalists' findings . . .

GG: Not if they can't address metaphysics, which they haven't for over 1,900 years!

PJ: . . . while naturalists are left only with their findings, which are necessarily limited.

GG: Well, given their progress in the last 200 years alone, it might be prudent to assume that the limitations aren't as great as you would like to paint them.

PJ: What do you think?

GG: I think I have written enough for now.

## THE END OF THE TOUR

Dear Greg:

I've been tracking BR's tour. This evening you're in Phoenix (uggh); tomorrow you're in LA (uggh!). I can imagine that seven gigs straight would be tiring. Do you mix up the sets, so you're not playing the exact same thing at each show?

Last evening I watched a local rugby match and then came home and read your vigorous response to my "challenging naturalism" note. The game and note were a perfect match.

One thing I like is that both of us believe that the other is mistaken about the nature of reality—much more interesting than politically correct relativism. At the same time, I see naturalistic investigation as complementary to theology, and you have said a few times that you are interested in seeing genuine evidence that could lend support to the concept of God. So there's room for two guys to work.

Why did you go to graduate school, anyway? Now that it's behind you, what do you think of it?

My Ph.D. dissertation defense was a bloodbath, mainly because no one on the panel knew what the dissertation was about. My advisor had died a few months earlier. So the ad hoc committee and I argued for two and a half hours over peripheral things. I hung tough and passed, but it was easily one of the worst experiences of my life.

Overall, I'm pretty cynical about the academy—especially the side of it that ignores students in favor of prestige and monetary awards.

Take care,
Preston

---

Dear Preston,

I have just returned to New York and I am fatigued. So fatigued, in fact, that the doctor has ordered three days of bed rest. It appears as though I picked up a virus on the plane flight home because my immune system was so worn out from seven shows in a row.

Yes, it is incredibly difficult to play that many shows in a row. I have a rule of three days on, one day off, three days on, one day off, on tour. We broke that rule because I allowed it. I thought that so many shows in one place might allow my body to heal each night because I didn't have to travel so much; we played in Arizona, Colorado and California. It wore me out nonetheless.

I have changed my views significantly on Los Angeles. I recently bought a house with my mom for her retirement. She moved back to our old neighborhood in the Valley, and now I stay there with her when I go to LA. I used to hate LA, but now I love it. I think it is because I don't feel trapped there anymore. No one can live there exclusively without growing tired of it. It is only because of my freedom to escape back to the pleasant confines of upstate New York that I love LA. My friends and family who live there are indispensable parts of me, so I regard LA as an important part of my life.

***If faith and reason are both gifts from God, they should play complementary, not conflicting, roles in our struggle to understand the world around us. . . . As a scientist and as a Christian, that is exactly what I believe. True knowledge comes only from a combination of faith and reason.***

**Kenneth R. Miller, cell biologist (1999)**

I wouldn't say you are necessarily mistaken about the nature of reality. But I believe this: There is only one reality (though people's personal responses to it will differ). The best way to understand it is through naturalism. Theology gives us little explanation of this reality, at least little explanation that anyone can believe if they know anything about how the world works.

I agree with you that "naturalistic investigation" can be "complementary to theology," but I can't say the reverse is true—that theology is complementary to naturalistic investigation. It is more important to know naturalism than to know theology if you want to understand how human beings and nature work.

I also agree that "there's room for two smart guys to work" with the ideas we've been discussing, but before that can happen we need to know what God is.

Sincerely,

Greg

## THE INEVITABILITY OF PEOPLE AND FOUNDATIONS FOR MORALITY

Dear Greg:

Take care of yourself. I hope you're feeling better soon. I know you must get tired of hearing nice things from fans, but I've been listening to BR's *The Gray Race* lately, and I had forgotten what an incredible album it is. "Them and Us" is excellent!

***For all its objectivity science, by definition, is a human construct, and offers no promise of final answers. We should, however, remind ourselves that we live in a Universe that seems strangely well suited for us. . . . More mysterious . . . is the attempt to explain the origins of sentience, such that the product of ultimately inanimate processes can come to understand both itself, its world, and . . . its (and thus our) strange sense of purpose.***

**Simon Conway Morris, paleontologist (2003)**

I'm reading an article in *U.S. News and World Report* about the view of Simon Conway Morris (Cambridge) that "the emergence of humans was inevitable." His new book is *Life's Solution: Inevitable Humans in a Lonely Universe.* You may know about this already—just thought I'd pass it along.

Get well. Enjoy the rest.

Peace,
Preston

Dear Preston,

Thanks for the tip on Simon Conway Morris. He was among the participants in my doctoral study. He is a paleontologist from the U.K. Paleontologists and botanists show the highest percentages of religiosity among all evolutionary biologists. This aroused my curiosity, so I talked about it with my master's degree advisor. We had lunch last week when I was in Phoenix, where he is now

***Wind back the tape of life [to prehistoric, prehuman times]; let it play again from an identical starting point, and the chance becomes vanishingly small that anything like human intelligence would grace the replay.***

***We are the offspring of history, and must establish our own paths in this most diverse and interesting of conceivable universes—one indifferent to our suffering, and therefore offering us maximal freedom to thrive, or to fail, in our own chosen way.***

**Stephen Jay Gould, evolutionary biologist (1989)**

retired, and he said to me "Why paleontologists? Why would they have the highest number of religious believers?" My advisor, a paleontologist who was trained by one of the greats of twentieth-century biology (A. S. Romer at Harvard), thinks it entirely possible that paleontologists in general are just not as smart as other evolutionary biologists.

Now, obviously there is a certain degree of humor in his arrogance and, indeed, some paleontologists are among the smartest of all biologists. You would have to know him to appreciate that, and he would never go "on record" as saying such a thing. But in the case of Simon Conway Morris, I believe he might be right.

It is completely inane to suggest, unless you are a theist, that the evolutionary process could somehow make humans inevitable. The unlikelihood of human inevitability has been brilliantly discussed by some of the best minds in modern biology, and convincingly so. Stephen Jay Gould wrote an excellent book on the unlikelihood that humans should exist *(Wonderful Life).*

To me, this makes human life all that much more precious! What a rare treat to be able to be part of this drama. That is a foundation for morality. A much better one than the theistic belief founded on the notion that we are predestined in the mind of some invisible agent.

Sincerely,
Greg

---

Dear Greg:

Today, on your advice, I requested (at the library) Wilson's *Consilience,* Huxley's *Religion with Revelation* and Smith's *Man and His Gods.* I'm looking forward to seeing what I learn from them.

You probably wrote that Morris is a "suspected theist" with tongue in cheek, but that does have, shall we say, an inquisitorial ring to it! In the *U.S. News* article, Morris claims to be a member of the Church of England.

But as you know, the idea that genuinely brilliant people can't be theists is beyond ludicrous. And the cliché that atheism is only for the supersmart is also junk, as the barely literate schoolboy skeptics who lounge in student centers mouthing weary anti-religion slogans prove.

The idea that "the unlikelihood that humans should exist . . . makes human life all that much more precious!" and that it's "a rare treat to be able to be part of this drama" are hard for me wrap my mind—or my psyche (in the Greek sense)—around. I understand what you mean, but I'm unable to muster the kind of faith you have that time + chance + randomness + an indifferent universe = "a foundation for morality." You seem to want to keep the "ethics" of Sermon on the Mount while chucking the person who delivered it.

***You have heard that it was said, "Love your neighbor and hate your enemy." But I tell you: Love your enemies and pray for those who persecute you. . . . If you love those who love you, what reward will you get?***

**Jesus, Sermon on the Mount, Matthew 5:43-46**

That's a bit like saying, "I like Graffin's lyrics but I have no use at all for him as a person." The lyrics and the person are inextricable.

If I saw the world the way naturalists do, I would agree more with some lyrics of yours: "It's our duty to be adversarial and free; our evolution didn't hinge on passivity." I think that I would conclude that Nietzsche was a prophet worth heeding.

Are you feeling better?

Peace,
Preston

***What is good? All that heightens the feeling of power in man, the will to power, power itself. What is bad? All that is born of weakness. What is happiness? The feeling that power is growing, that resistance is overcome.***

**Friedrich Nietzsche, philosopher and writer (1895)**

Dear Preston,

I am not feeling better yet. I am in the third day of what the doctor said would be three days of hell.

I must confess that you probably have thought much more about this word "morality" than I have. That is likely due to the fact that a theological education places a huge emphasis on that word and the sacredness associated with it.

Evolutionary biology spends very little time talking about morality. But from the work I did in my dissertation interviews, and from some of E. O. Wilson's writing, it is clear that morality can be understood from a biological perspective and need not be as sacred as the theologians once believed. In fact, Smith's book *Man and His Gods* nicely illustrates how morality is functional and an epiphenomenon of culture. It has changed drastically throughout recorded history.

My religion, which is of course as yet undefined and totally unpopular, accepts morality as a set of prescribed rules that came not from a supernatural being and his mysterious wisdom, but rather came from a recognition of human behavior. We humans can recognize our own behavior and we can codify it. We are smart beings who can characterize good and bad behavior and relate it to how it makes us feel (good or bad).

I don't think anyone feels good after killing someone, even in revenge. I can only empathize in the sense that once, in grade school, I punched a kid and hurt him bad, and even though he was a bully he cried, which proved he really wasn't so tough after all—hence, not much of a bully. The fact that our emotions have evolved this mechanism of conscience lends weight to the belief that our emotions have some social significance and play an important role in our social interactions.

Very little work has been done on this, but it is perfectly easy to do it. Ask kids how they feel when they hurt someone, for instance. If it can be demonstrated that conscience is natural—not taught, not learned, but there from the start—then it is reasonable to treat it as we would treat any biological trait, like hemoglobin, and it is reasonable to assume that it is an evolutionary adaptation in some way to social life. So, your difficulty in wrapping your head around my statement in my last note comes from the fact that you were taught a much different concept of morality than I was. Perhaps we need a different word. I know this: much more data needs to be collected!

Homer Smith wrote nicely. You will appreciate him, I think. I am enjoying *Brideshead Revisited* immensely in my hours of bed rest. I am glad that I bought the miniseries. Thank you for the suggestion. By the way, *Consilience* is excellent. However, Wilson won the Pulitzer Prize for a book called *On Human Nature*, which is also very important for its theological implications.

Catch you later,

Greg

Dear Greg:

I'm bummed that you're still feeling bad. I'll send a prayer up into the indifferent universe for you. I'll add Wilson's *On Human Nature* to my order of yesterday.

***The human species can change its own nature. What will it choose?***

**E. O. Wilson, biologist (1978)**

Just this morning (it's about 7 a.m. now) I was thinking of our exchanges and connecting them unintentionally—in the weird way the brain does things—with an exchange between Charles and Julia toward the end of the *Brideshead* book/miniseries. It has to do with what should happen at the deathbed of Julia's father. . . .

I have to run to work.

All the best,
Preston

---

Dear Preston,

I must confess that I didn't finish reading your last e-mail. The nanosecond that I saw you hint at "Charles and Julia" I closed the message because I feared you were giving some information that I haven't yet reached in the story.

But thanks for the prayer. I think last night in the middle of my slumber I felt an indescribable tingling feeling in the netherparts. That must have been God letting me know he had been notified of my infirmity!

Sincerely,
Greg

Dear Greg:

I was thinking that I shouldn't say anything about . . .

Anyway, I hoped you enjoyed that tingling. At our age, all such experiences are blessings. Actually, when it comes to the netherparts, God's résumé is pretty impressive—the imposition of temporary sterility, orchestrating a virgin birth, etc. In the Old Testament there's a book called Song of Songs (or Canticles). God's never mentioned in the book—it's just good fleshy literature. You should check it out if the tingling returns.

***May the wine go straight to my lover,***
***flowing gently over lips and teeth. . . .***
***Come, my lover, let us go to the countryside,***
***let us spend the night in the villages.***

**Song of Songs 7:9-11**

Here's the part of the previous note you missed: We agree that morality generally conceived comes naturally to people. James Q. Wilson's book *The Moral Sense* does a great job of accumulating social scientific research to show that this is so. Wilson sees that, relative to their counterparts, religious folks tend to volunteer more, they give more to charity, they tend to share household chores more, they have more stable relationships, they take fewer illicit drugs, they kill themselves less often, etc.

***If all people were equal before the law and in the eyes of God, all had some claim to consideration and equitable treatment.***

**James Q. Wilson, social theorist (1993)**

Anyway, I want to pass by you some comparisons I make between our respective faiths. These thoughts have occurred to me while reading E. O. Wilson's *Consil-*

*ience* and while thinking about your earlier notes.

***Reasonable faiths.*** Both Christian theism and materialistic naturalism are reasonable because they work. Since its beginnings, Christian faith has changed lives for the better—murderers have become saints, drug addicts have become social workers, the excessively proud have adjusted to reality, etc. Materialistic naturalism has also helped to make lives better in that it has rescued people from brainless (as opposed to genuine) religion and has spurred medical and scientific discovery. The question is, which of these two faiths is the more reasonable?

***Brutality.*** Both Christians and naturalist-materialists are responsible for atrocities—e.g., pogroms perpetrated by Christians in the late Middle Ages, the gutlessness of the majority of Christians in Nazi Germany, the death squads of France's anti-Christian revolutionaries, and the mass murder of the twentieth century's officially atheistic regimes. The question is, which of these faiths is least likely to lend support to brutality?

***The terror of 1936-8 [in the Soviet Union] was an almost uniquely devastating blow inflicted by a government on its own population, and the charges against the millions of victims were almost without exception entirely false. Stalin personally ordered, inspired and organized the operation.***

**Robert Conquest, historian and political writer (1991)**

***Faith.*** Both Christian theists and materialistic naturalists exercise faith. Theists have faith in a God they cannot see directly, though they can speak to him, and they perceive that they can gain guidance from him; they sense his presence; they can see his work in their lives; and they can love him and be angry at him. Among thoughtful theists at least, this faith isn't "blind"; it's based on a relationship, albeit one not precisely paralleled by any other. It is based on an experiential knowledge that, in good cases, is in accord with Christian intellectual tradition. It's true that, unfortunately, many Christians have little insight into Christian tradition; their "experiences" are rooted in emotion—songs sung at camp, the hype of a talented preacher and so on.

Materialists put their faith in the idea that the vast majority of people who have lived, and who live now, are fundamentally mistaken about some of life's most basic questions. Against the vast majority of people, materialists believe that no ultimate meaning exists in a nonmaterialistic world, because there is no nonmaterialistic world. Also against the vast majority of people, materialists believe that there is no use in looking for solutions, or partial solutions, to the human condition in spiritual sources. (The philosopher John Kekes warns readers against falling for the "metaphysical temptation.")

Positively, materialists believe that naturalistic causes for the most complex and seemingly mysterious phenomena will (or can) be found, given enough time and resources. Since the future is unknowable, and since mystery continues to pervade human life despite naturalism's achievements heretofore, this belief is precisely that—a belief nurtured by the faith of a relatively small sect known especially to gather in science departments at universities, mainly in Europe and in other Western or Westernized societies. (Heretics in these departments often have a tough time.)

***Reality is a multi-layered unity. I can perceive another person as an aggregation of atoms, an open biochemical system in interaction with the environment, a specimen of homo sapiens, an object of beauty, someone whose needs deserve my respect and compassion, a brother for whom Christ died. All are true and all mysteriously co-inhere in that one person.***

**John Polkinghorne, physicist and theologian (1986)**

Christian faith has no problem absorbing the discoveries of naturalists. As some Christians put it, "It's God's world," so whatever seems to be true about the world, as borne out by science, is welcomed, or should be, because it tells us about God's world.

On the other hand, materialistic naturalists, as a matter of faith, must protect their creed from impurities: No deities allowed.

All the best,
Preston

Dear Preston,

I commend you on your summary of the two faiths. But I don't think using the criterion of a faith "working" is useful. Remember, there are tribes in Africa who believe the moon lies just beyond the seeable horizon and is actually made of a cheeselike substance. This belief "works" well for them—it fits into their creation myths somehow, and they have no need to test it. But such a belief is an absurdity.

***Tell me, where is the love?***
***In a careless creation***
***When there's no "above"***
***There's no justice***
***Just a cause and a cure***
***And a bounty of suffering***
***It seems we all endure***
***And what I'm frightened of***
***Is that they call it "God's love"***

**Greg Graffin, "God's Love,"** ***The Empire Strikes First*** **(2004)**

Many Christian beliefs don't "work" at all. I saw a lecture last week by a very good paleontologist from an Ivy League university. I admire his bravery, although when someone is brave for a lost cause, all I can admire is the bravery. He stated outright that he is a theist and believes all of evolution is driven forward by "God's love."

At the end of the lecture I promptly said, in front of the entire audience, "That explanation of evolution doesn't acknowledge all the data. It ignores all the suffering from biological agents: predation, infection, starvation, psychological maladies of humans, etc. How, by any stretch of the imagination, can you convince us that this has anything to do with 'love'?" Of course his answer, basically, was, "The ways of God are mysterious and human suffering is a 'big' question."

In other words, the central problem with theistic faith is that it can't give a good explanation for so much obvious suffering, not only in humans, but everywhere a biologist looks. We think the forest is healthy and full of perfectly adapted organisms, a wonderful example of God's wisdom. Look more carefully, and we see that virtually every tree is infested with parasites, and the parasites themselves are infested with bacterial parasites. Instead of thriving, the entire community is just getting by in a precariously balanced equilibrium that serves the parasite as much as the host.

How can this have anything to do with a loving and caring creator? How can children suffering from malnutrition be any evidence of God's love? What about genetic diseases that are passed from unknowing parents to their completely innocent newborn baby? What kind of love is that? Would this be some kind of theological test for parents?

Naturalists have an explanation for understanding suffering. In that sense alone, it is more useful than theism. Take brutality. Brutality is going to happen, no matter what faith is dominant. I am convinced of that. This is my way of cutting Christianity some slack, actually, because it has been the dominant worldview for the rise of our modern world. It leads the way in fostering brutal death and misery. But if some other form of belief were in power, I believe similar atrocities would pervade our history.

Atrocities are a part of human civilization and are the result of ignorance about human nature. Until naturalistic investigation, there was no way to understand human nature. But that will change in the coming centuries. Human behavior will be better understood and, hopefully, suffering will be minimized.

As long as Christian theology has no satisfying answer to human suffering, it is at a terrible disadvantage. That is why so many intellectuals have moved away from it as a belief system, and even the religious intelligentsia offer an uncomfortable explanation of suffering: "God's ways are mysterious." It simply isn't a satisfying intellectual explanation. Nobody, not even a child, sits well with that; they merely give in to the fear of authority and the weight of history.

Naturalism depends on science, which in turn is anti-authoritarian because any momentary new discovery will overturn the entire theoretical structure. But it has to be repeatable. Do an experiment. Repeat it. It has powers of convincing and it makes you feel good! Especially when it solves difficult puzzles about the world. Knowledge is the cure for the disgruntled.

On the issue you raised of what the "vast majority" of people who have lived have believed: It is not a prudent line of reasoning to say that because the "vast majority of people who have ever lived believe in so and so" you must then concede an important fact. The people in the past were far more ignorant than we are. If you can't concede that point then I will go no further and you can chuck out all that I have ever written because you are not acknowledging any increase in knowledge from the ascent of science.

The people of the past knew nothing about neurons or brain development. (By the past, I mean, say, from the time of Christ to the nineteenth century). It is no wonder they couldn't conceive of the concepts that are now before us.

The child's brain develops and is highly susceptible to stories during the first seven years. There is a strong tendency, as the neurons are creating their interconnections, for a child to absorb the beliefs of her parent. The child creates a worldview in this manner and modifies it (I believe only slightly, but it could be drastically—research remains to be undertaken) through later education. Now if the only stories around prior to the scientific age were stories of religion, there was no way the societies of the past could understand or promote any alternatives. Today, even though alternatives exist, most kids are still exposed to religious creation stories and religious morality stories. So it is no wonder most people who have ever lived believe in God: They haven't had any other education!

But we find ourselves at an interesting place in history. Due to mass media, more and more kids are being exposed to science. More young brains are being exposed to naturalistic explanations. (Think of the Discovery Channel for instance, or Bill Nye the Science Guy—a Carl Sagan student from here at Cornell.)

Most often, religious storytelling occurs in households with religious backgrounds. At the same time, modern kids learn about science. The result is that science and religion get implanted in the kids' brains, creating a muddled view of both. Look around our society and, behold, that is exactly what we see. The questionnaires and surveys need to be done, but I think the average modern American has a very muddled view of both science and religion and mixes tenets from both to create their worldview.

I mean, think of all the people who call themselves Christians and put their faith in the Bible but at the same moment acknowledge the scientific fact that humans descended from apelike ancestors? I think the average American citizen is like this. See what I mean? Muddled! The facts of naturalism are too powerful for people to ignore, but they haven't had time, or haven't had the need, to think deeply about how that conflicts with the tenets and implications of traditional theology.

We are at a transitional period in the intellectual history of the United States (and perhaps the world). The average citizen depends less on, and reads less of, the Bible while at the same time is more knowledgeable about the natural world than ever before. This will continue, and will probably move theology even farther to the back burner. How many kids today say, "I want to be a Jesuit when I grow up," or "I want to be a nun," or "I want to be the pope"? Compare that to the kids who say "I want to be a marine biologist," "I want to be a doctor," "I want to be an astronaut."

It seems that things are changing before our eyes. But first, we have to unmuddle the thinking inherent in the two systems (theology and naturalism). Theology benefits from muddle. Science cannot work with muddle. Experiments depend on clarity and are free from "noise." Theology can continue to assert itself in the face of muddle because at its core is the concept that keeps all its followers in a state of confusion: "The ways of God are mysterious."

Sincerely,

Greg

## THE FALL

Dear Greg:

I am being thoroughly irresponsible by writing. I should be reading in preparation for a public lecture I have to give in two weeks—but I won't be able to write again till tomorrow evening.

If the Ivy League paleontologist said that evolution is the fruit of "God's love," then I applaud you for challenging him, and I wish I could have been there to challenge him alongside you, albeit from a different perspective.

If you go back and read your description of the world (parasites, etc.), then you pretty much have described my view, and you may be surprised to know that your view is (it seems to me) much closer to a biblical "perspective" than the one apparently pronounced last week at the lecture you attended. (Pardon me for a second as I turn on *The Gray Race*. . . .)

The traditional Christian view is that all the world—all of nature—is warped as a consequence of the Fall, i.e., man's rebellion against God.

***INQUIRY BOX***

**When Christians refer to the Fall, they are usually referring to an event described early in the book of Genesis: Adam and Eve lost their moral perfection as a result of their disobedience to God. They ate from the one tree in the Garden of Eden that God commanded them not to. Paradise was lost.**

**Some Christians interpret this story literally. Others say that the story of the Fall describes, in a literary way that is still divinely inspired, a basic truth about human beings: You can put them in paradise, give them everything they want, and they will wreck it.**

**C. S. Lewis, a professor of English at Oxford and Cambridge, wrote that as a result of the Fall, people have become "ill-adapted to the universe." Another scholar, David Lyle Jeffrey, suggests that the story in Genesis points to the "fragmentation," "alienation" and "estrangement" that people often feel. They feel this way because they are out of sync with the way things should be and the way God wants things to be.**

**Does it seem to you that people are "fallen"? Does life seem alien to people? If very few people like being lonely, why is loneliness so common? Does it seem to you that people do things to sabotage their own plans? Why would people do such things? Why do people want the world to be better but do things to make it worse?**

I know you don't believe that, but at least that view takes the nature of the real world seriously.

But the longer I live in American Christendom, where anxieties are medicated with TV, junk food and political slogans, the more I realize that American Christians don't really want to take the idea of fallenness seriously.

The view expressed last week in your lecture hall

comes from a well-fed, upper-middle-class Western Christian apparently cut off from the tradition he purports to stand in. I don't know him, and I can't criticize him directly, but common these days among Christians is the type of evangelist who turns God into a jolly guy who just wants to be your pal. I keep looking for something in the Bible—and in the mass of Christian intellectual tradition—to justify this essentially American view, and I keep coming up short. Only one biblical book, Job, deals seriously, explicitly and relentlessly with evil (natural and human), and when Job asks God to explain himself, God basically tells him to put a cork in it.

***Then the LORD answered Job out of the storm. He said:***
***"Who is this that darkens my counsel***
***with words without knowledge? . . .***
***"Where were you when I laid the earth's foundation?"***
**Job 38:1-4**

For many years I've advocated that Christian theologians abandon the project of finding a comforting explanation for evil, especially suffering inflicted on the innocent (e.g., infants dying of malnutrition). The effort has been going on for centuries and, so far as I can see, it has failed. There is no comforting explanation, and the "God's ways are mysterious" line is a vapid and dangerous cliché—useful, perhaps, at funerals but not in the cut and thrust of daily life.

In a certain sense it may be true: there is a lot of mystery in life—in relationships, in questions concerning the "mind," in the fact that so often many people (like me) never seem to learn from others' mistakes. But practically speaking, that statement isn't very helpful, and it certainly doesn't answer any serious questions.

***When most people scan the world for signs of God it is not to its scientific orderliness that they look. Rather it is such matters as the incidence of debilitating and destructive disease that concern them. The randomly imposed burdens of unmerited suffering seem to many to call in question assertions that the world is in the care of a loving God. . . . At the deepest level I believe that the only possible answer is to be found in the darkness and dereliction of the cross, where Christianity asserts that in that lonely figure hanging there we see God himself opening his arms to embrace the bitterness of the strange world he has made.***

**John Polkinghorne, physicist and theologian (1986)**

When I was in the Navy I saw a great deal of pointless evil—young girls trapped in brothels, a filthy legless boy begging for coins outside a U.S. military base, kids diving for pennies in a feces-ridden "river." Nothing I can think of could ever justify this suffering, and if God orchestrated all of it, then the only moral thing to do (as Camus suggested) is to revolt against him.

The Christian view is that God doesn't want the world to be like this; and when the curtains fall—when he ends it (perhaps by allowing people to annihilate themselves, perhaps by waiting for the sun to burn out)—the world to follow won't be like this.

In the meantime, what we must do is alleviate as much suffering as we can by, for example, helping people to give up self-destructive behaviors, by conserving the world's resources, by promoting education, by helping neighbors, etc. Here's where you and I are firm allies (though I guess we might squabble over the contents of what should be taught).

***The whole range of human miseries, from restlessness and estrangement through shame and guilt to the agonies of daytime television—all of them tell us that things in human life are not as they ought to be.***

**Cornelius Plantinga Jr., theologian (1995)**

I still think the Christian response to evil is better than the naturalist's. People look around, see the evil and suffering and think that something is warped, something is out of whack. The Christian responds by agreeing, yes, the world is warped—here's why, and here's what you can hope for.

***We know that the whole creation has been groaning as in the pains of childbirth right up to the present time. Not only so, but we ourselves, who have the firstfruits of the Spirit, groan inwardly as we wait eagerly for our adoptions as sons, the redemption of our bodies.***

**St. Paul, Letter to the Romans 8:22-23**

The naturalist, it seems, can't really say that the world (excluding human behavior) is warped. The world is just the way it is. All the pain in the animal kingdom, the combat in the insect world, the parasites in the trees—it's all just natural and there's no use feeling good or bad about it. That's the naturalist's answer, but it's not a satisfying answer. It's even less satisfying than "God's ways are mysterious."

Well, I planned just on writing a couple paragraphs. My responses to four other points you raised will have to wait. As you're telling me right now (via my stereo speaker), "everything must cease"—including this e-mail.

Take care, bud.
Preston

---

Dear Preston,

I really appreciate your clarification. Your answer is a lot more satisfying than "the ways of God are mysterious." But I must take on your suggestion that a naturalist would answer "there's no use feeling good or bad" about suffering. A naturalist would acknowledge that sufferings exists, feel terrible about it, and search for a way to cure it!

I would add that any God who is all-powerful, who presides

---

***The road is narrow the horizon wide,***

***And they say what's waiting on the other side,***

***It's so rewarding, the ultimate prize.***

***But what good is something if you can't have it until you die?***

***Desperate, tenacious, clinging like a grain of sand,***

***Watching its foundation wash away, wash away,***

***Drunk with the assertions they know they can't defend,***

***Confident that they might live again.***

**Greg Graffin, "Live Again—The Fall of Man"** ***The Empire Strikes First*** **(2004)**

---

over a religion that claims effective communication with him, and who ignores the suffering of babies is a total hard-ass for punishment. All because Adam ate a f****** apple? Wait, Eve ate the apple; it was womanhood, of course, that ruined humankind! Give us a break, big guy in the sky!

Problem: Adam and Eve didn't even exist. So some australopithecine must have eaten something to piss God off.

So what is the basis for the fall of man? You will have to wait until the next BR album for that answer. A new song to appear on it is called "Fall of Man."

Needless to say, it will have my bias. Good luck on your lecture.

Sincerely,
Greg

---

Dear Greg:

If the lecture I'm supposed to be preparing for bombs, it's your fault.

Your note makes a serious point in a very funny way—or at least I thought it was funny. I was smiling all day.

I agree that if all the car accidents that took place today happened because an australopithecine gnawed on a piece of fruit, then that would be pretty amazing, not to mention unfair. Some Christians insist on reading the Eden story with no room for interpretation. But so far as I can tell, the literary genre of the text (not to mention the ideas of basic fairness, which people got from somewhere) calls for thoughtful reflection.

What we see in the story of the Fall are human beings

blowing an opportunity to live good, even perfect, lives. What we also see is God letting people make their own choices—if they want to wreck their lives and the lives of their children, he'll let them.

***Our wealth is great, but our economy has been seriously damaged by the greed, selfishness, and shortsightedness that have become its ruling principles. . . . We are . . . completing the economic destruction of our rural and agricultural communities. We are destroying our farmlands, our forests, our water sources. We are polluting the air, the water, the land.***

**Wendell Berry, farmer and writer (1993)**

We see this sort of thing all the time—the Fall is repeated every day. People know they should exercise, but they don't. They know they shouldn't eat so much garbage, but they do. They know they should help the needy, but they don't. They know they shouldn't toast their brains sitting in front of the TV hour after hour, but they do. They know they should foster trust by being reliable, but they don't. They know that lying destroys relationships and that they shouldn't do it, but they do.

***Blessed are the merciful, for they will be shown mercy.***

**Jesus, Sermon on the Mount, Matthew 5:7**

Every sane person would agree that life would be better if everyone could abide by the Sermon on the Mount.

Every sane person would also agree that the chances of that happening in this world are zero. Not because it's an inherent impossibility, but because people are self-destructive. That's the Fall—repeated daily.

Much of the world's "natural evil" isn't really natural. Kids starve in Africa because the scumbags who run their countries hoard food sent by aid agencies. Poverty and crises in the "developing world" are increasing because people who can't feed or care for the kids they already

***Even in its most basic form [in Genesis chapters 2 and 3], the story of the Fall not only speaks of the first man and the first woman naked before each other and God . . . it also faces the mystery of the perverse will that listens to the voice of the beast rather than the voice of God, and chooses death rather than life.***

**Dennis Danielson, professor of English (1992)**

have keep having more children. The climatic calamities we can expect as the rain forests continue to be ravaged will be our own fault.

There is, of course, much suffering in the world that has no relation whatever to human action, and that is difficult to account for if one assumes that God is just.

***Why do you look at the speck of sawdust in your brother's eye and pay no attention to the plank in your own eye? How can you say to your brother, "Let me take the speck out of your eye," when all the time there is a plank in your own eye? You hypocrite, first take the plank out of your own eye, and then you will see clearly to remove the speck from your brother's eye.***

**Jesus, Sermon on the Mount, Matthew 7:3-5**

But I don't see any conflict between the belief that God is just and the recognition that people are responsible for the vast majority of the suffering people experience. God is all-powerful in the sense that he is much more powerful than we—and people will have to give an account to him for what they did in life. But he isn't so powerful as to change the basic rules of the game: People are free agents.

Jesus provides us with a behavioral regimen that would rescue us (the Sermon on the Mount)—but neither you nor I nor anyone else (even the holy saints) will follow it day in and out.

And now I turn to washing the dishes.

Peace,
Preston

## FREE WILL

Dear Preston,

I appreciate your answer. In response, I can only offer this, one of my favorite quotes, which describes the heart of my beliefs and provides an empirical observation of humankind's intellectual history:

> The most astonishing logical paradox ever to be cherished by man is presented in the circumstance that the theologists, convinced that God in his omnipotence had predetermined the fate of every man, and in his omniscience had from the beginning of time foreseen that fate, should yet hold to the belief that he nevertheless holds every man responsible for

> his action, rewarding him either with eternal beatitude or eternal punishment. For theology the invention of free will to which culpability could be assigned only formalized the complete abandonment of reason in order to keep the system in operation. (Homer Smith, *Man and His Gods*)

I couldn't have put it better myself. Perhaps the world is based on an astonishing logical paradox. But I don't believe in free will, and I don't think theology can survive without it.

***In Niger, a desert country twice the size of Texas, most of the 11 million people live on a dollar a day. Forty percent of children are underfed, and one out of four dies before turning 5. And that's when things are normal. Throw in a plague of locusts, and a familiar picture emerges: skeletal babies, distended bellies, people too famished to brush the flies from their faces. . . . [Niger's] desert is getting bigger and drought is unrelenting.***

**Todd Pitman, journalist (2005)**

Of course ignorance is lenient, and if we close our eyes to science, or we fail to learn about biological phenomena (such as neuroscience) we can readily believe that we have special powers of free will. We "feel" free. Unless, of course, you are among the large proportion of humans on this planet who are seriously suffering.

Theology depends on such ignorance.

Sincerely,

Greg

Dear Greg:

A former student went out and bought a bunch of BR CDs, so you owe me.

I agree with Homer Smith that it's problematic to say that either God predetermined all things or that he perfectly foreknows all things (so that all that can happen is what he already knows will happen) and that people are still responsible for their actions. I think both views are troublesome: I'm a theological "libertarian," and while I won't bore you with a dissertation on that, suffice it to say that I really think that people are free and are involved in shaping the future.

> ***God bestows a certain autonomy not only to human beings, as Christian theology has long recognized, but also on the natural order as such to develop in ways that God chooses not to control in detail. God allows a degree of open-endedness and flexibility in nature, and this becomes that natural, structural basis for the flexibility of conscious organisms and . . . possibly for the freedom . . . of persons.***
>
> **Arthur R. Peacocke, biochemist and priest (2000)**

I know you agree with me on that (excluding the God part) because that view shows up in your songs, especially on *The New America.*

I want to learn about your view of free will, or the extent to which you don't believe in it. I'd guess that we agree that temperament, personality, genetics and so on predispose us to act in certain ways; that environment shapes how we think and behave; that emotions, interests and drives have to do with brain and body wiring and chemistry.

***Follow me to the future's distant shore***
***Vagary needn't haunt us anymore***
***And now it's time to set the agenda, learn the past,***
***make it last***
***Share the wealth, hold your fire, conserve life,***
***make it right***
***Kill the hate, negotiate***
***There will be a way.***

**Greg Graffin, "There Will Be a Way,"** ***The New America*** **(2000)**

I am writing to you now, and not doing something else, for reasons rooted in my psychology, which is to say in the neurons in my brain. But I could have chosen not to write to you at this time. It's nearly 10 p.m.; I want to get up at 5:15 a.m. to go to the gym. The longer I write, the less likely it is that I'll get up—I feel some tension about my decision to write. But I am writing. Surely you'd agree that I am exercising my free will at this moment?

And a related question: In theological determinism there's a teleology—things are heading in a definite direction that cannot be derailed. (I don't believe this, but many do.) What is the deterministic naturalist's teleology?

And if people aren't really free, why would they "feel" free? That doesn't make sense!

Peace,
Preston

Dear Preston,

We have ventured onto ground that is one of the major interests of my advisor, William B. Provine. He's a historian of science and is writing a book on the implications of evolution, and I just finished commenting on his chapter on free will. He is the expert and if he wasn't so burdened this semester with teaching evolution, I would pass along your e-mail to him and let him explain (he is masterful at explanation).

There is something I might not have confessed to you before. I believe human beings would be much, much happier if they studied biology. All intellectual questions revolve around biology, whether we admit it or not. It is pathetic that biology is treated as an elective science and we are "taught" math as if it is the most important thing to master. Much strife occurs because the average citizen is completely in the dark about how life works.

Free will is one of those questions that is directly affected by biology. If someone is ignorant of biology, ignorant of what is going on biologically to produce feelings of "freedom," it is difficult to move forward in the discussion. Much literature on this topic has been awkwardly advanced by people who confuse the issue because they know nothing about biology. Then the reply always comes, "Well, what does knowledge have to do with whether we are free or not?" or "You can't tell me I'm not free just because you know more about how the brain works" and on and on. My reply: "Yes, I can." In my interviews with him, Richard Dawkins put it this way: "The illusion of free will is so powerful that we might as well assume we have it." He said this as an off-handed comment but, indeed, he believes we do not have free will.

***Brains evolved the capacity to communicate with other brains by means of language and cultural traditions. But the new milieu of cultural tradition opens up new possibilities for self-replicating entities. . . . These new replicators, which I call memes to distinguish them from genes, can propagate themselves from brain to brain, from brain to book, from brain to computer, from computer to computer.***

**Richard Dawkins, evolutionary biologist (1996)**

Feelings are traits that evolve just like the opposable thumb. Thoughts and ideas, however, might not be adaptations at all. A meme is just an idea or a thought process (brain function) that spreads throughout a population.

For instance, the idea that we should wash our hands after we go to the bathroom. That is an idea that got started because in the days before sanitary life, people associated disease with touching our genitalia. Indeed even today it's not hard to find companies that sell disinfectants perpetuating this meme, and there have been very few studies citing data that washing hands five times a day has anything to do with disease prevention. It is, in the words of my former advisor, Peter Vaughn, social medicine. Dawkins would call this a meme, an idea that has spread. Since it has no ill side effects it continues, even though it probably has no medical benefit either.

A side note to memes: Going against them could create social ostracism, which would have a deleterious effect on one's mental health, so it is a fine line.

The major point to recognize is that memes can come from anywhere, a suggestion somewhere in the past, an urban myth, a shocking event. But once a meme gets spread, it is very hard to eliminate it.

The feeling of freedom is such a meme, in my view. (I am not sure if my advisor, who is much more expert on this matter, has ever discussed this with me. But I think he would agree with me.) There is ample reinforcement of this meme, both in history (wars fought over freedom), and in our immediate cultural surrounding (in the land of the free). An excellent intellectual achievement would be an analysis of how this meme has developed through time.

Just this weekend, while waiting for a subway train in NYC, my girlfriend and I were discussing how filthy and disgusting the trains and platforms are. Millions of bits of bubble gum everywhere, grime and spit every step, cigarette butts at every turn. Why does this happen? Because people think, "Hey, its a free country." That's right—they shirk any sense of responsibility because they believe they are free to do whatever they want to do. Now, I agree they could justify this bad behavior even if they thought they had no free will. But let's face it, freedom rules the day, and it is the dominant meme that allows this behavior.

Remember, we are talking about a feeling here, a process in the brain that brings about a certain behavior. It is impossible for people to understand how mechanical all this is in the absence of biological knowledge. So when they hear that all organisms are determined by heredity and environment, they have no idea what that means. They treat such a statement with skepticism. Indeed, even many biologists don't appreciate the complexity involved in the word *environment.* They are used to controlling environmental conditions in their laboratory experiments. But it is clear that environmental determinants are extremely complex and have a time dimension as well.

Hereditary factors are also extremely complex—over 80,000 genes interacting with each other and with the extracellular environments. It is a very, very complicated matter that we've only just begun to figure out in any way. So until more is understood—and don't underestimate how fast we are accumulating knowledge about genetics and environment—it will not surprise me when people object to the statement that they are very complicated robots with the retort, "F*** you, I feel free. I live in America, therefore I am free."

I have started to challenge myself on the idea that you touched on near the end of your last note—the idea that "I am writing this now, and I could be doing something else, but I'm not, I am writing instead." I have started to think more along these lines: "I am doing this now, so some set of appropriate conditions must have come up to compel my brain to make me do this." We think we are aware of all the conditions that lead to our behavior. That is just human arrogance. In fact, even though our brains are the most elaborate computing and sensing devices, our consciousness cannot adequately monitor all the subtle stimuli that influence behavior. So we are conscious that we are doing something and we reason with ourselves about what must motivate this behavior, when in fact we do not know.

This is how I can feel compassionate toward criminals (even if I don't excuse them) and why I vehemently oppose punishment (I favor rehabilitation and re-education), and I strongly oppose the death penalty (deterrents don't work after all, and if you believe what I outlined above it is no wonder they don't work). If we cannot consciously make sense of the stimuli it is no wonder we have the illusion of free will.

Sincerely,

Greg

## FREEDOM AND ENVIRONMENT

Dear Greg:

Now it's my turn to be sick—aches, pains, clouded brain, stomach in disarray, etc. But as always, your most recent note is provocative. Here are my thoughts:

Of course you're right that "all intellectual questions revolve around biology." Given a certain type of brain injury, I could cease to have the capacity to feel love for my daughter; given a certain unbalance in brain chemistry, I could come to think that I am Napoleon or the lead singer of Bad Religion.

But I think it can't be correct to say that behavior is just the stuff of biology. Chinese people see the world in a very different way from Oklahomans, who are themselves different from Icelanders. The behaviors and views different people hold are obviously arrived at via biological routes (external stimuli affecting the central and peripheral nervous systems), but the biological routes are themselves affected by external forces (e.g., heavy TV consumption alters the development of a young child's brain). To put the thought in a clumsy way, ideas transmitted through the air are free of biology until they take hold and shape how a person thinks, which in turn may in subtle ways change how a brain is "wired."

If biology alone explained all of human behavior, then wouldn't one expect people everywhere to be basically the same since, with minor exceptions (such as vulnerability to sickle cell anemia), human biology is the same? New Yorkers' belief that it's a mark of freedom to spit all over the place in the subway doesn't exist in Singapore. If behavior only bubbled upward from biology, and if New Yorkers' and Singaporeans' biology is the same, then wouldn't one expect the memes to be the same? The different memes Singaporeans and New Yorkers possess couldn't exist apart from biology, but it doesn't seem that they can be explained only by biology.

Memes house themselves in biology (more clumsy language) but also float in the air (clumsy!) and are sometimes rejected. The subway behavior you describe exemplifies a rejection of an earlier meme—at a time not so long ago New York's subways weren't so disgusting. I'm amazed when I see pictures of New York subways taken in the 1940s and all the men are wearing coats and ties!

Monozygotic twins are quite similar, but there are always personality differences. If one monozygotic twin develops schizophrenia, the other is quite likely to do the same, but this isn't a given, especially if the twins are raised in different environments.

Here's what makes no sense to me about your position: Let's assume you're right, that humans are basically highly sophisticated "robots" and they are that way just because that's the way they are (as a result of a purely materialistic evolution). Then logically it wouldn't make sense for people to want to resist this idea. People don't get upset about the existence of trees. They don't get upset about the existence of oxygen. They don't get upset about water. They know that insects serve a purpose. Yet people instinctively (I use that word intentionally) reject the idea that they are completely predetermined, strictly material robots. Even the people I know who believe in strict theological determinism don't ordinarily talk as if they do; they say "maybe," "perhaps" and "fortunately" as much as everyone else.

***There is an intuition that is difficult to shake. I refer to the deep sense that human behavior is not entirely shaped by causal factors but is partially self-determining. It is an intuition that people hold in practice even when they deny it intellectually. For example, we hold others responsible for their actions. . . . We do not consider the fact that a person holds a different viewpoint than ours as something they were predestined to do; and we exhort one another because we assume that people can change their ways.***

**Clark H. Pinnock, theologian (2001)**

But if people really had no free will, it wouldn't make sense for them to get upset about it. Their robotness would be as natural to them as wood or dirt or cucumbers.

Peace,
Preston

Dear Preston,

Usually your responses have more depth than the last one. With this last note you have followed in the tradition of philosophers who have never studied biology, raising issues that clearly reveal that fact. You have made an incorrect assumption about my last note. It seems you think that I somehow do not appreciate the importance of environment. Please let me address that tedious issue, only because it seems I wasn't clear enough in my last note.

The fact that I think we are extremely complex robots doesn't mean I ignore the importance of the environment. By "environment" I mean all cultural and organismic, as well as physical, determining influences on an organism's behavior. Even slight differences in experience can produce different behaviors from identical twins. This begins from moment one. One of the twins is first out of the uterus. The second twin's earliest experience of the world is the presence of another being who was there before him or her. This has an effect on the developing neurons in the brain.

Every slight difference adds up to different personalities. But of course, the more closely related genotypes possess more similar behaviors than distantly related ones. This subtlety I just pointed to is commonly in the thoughts of biologists, but as you reveal, is met with incredulity or simple ignorance from people who don't think about biology. The lack of consideration given to biology also is the reason that so many people reject any notion that we might be robots. They have no idea what such a world would look like since they can't imagine a robot that's as clever and complicated as a person.

I know that we who make such claims bear the burden to educate. But such an education is easier to accomplish today than it was 100 years ago; more people would understand the explanation today. In 100 years it will be even easier to educate people on such a topic, because even more will be revealed from neurobiology and behavior.

This concept you advance, that memes (ideas) are just "floating in the wind" is very strange. Ideas come from the physical process of human minds. Some human advances an idea and it either catches on (by humans repeating it) or it dies out (by humans failing to repeat it). It doesn't persist if humans don't repeat it somehow. That is why Asians and Westerners have such different worldviews. The Asian memes, which have uniquely interacted with Eastern people through history, don't translate in the West because unique historical ideas here have served to shape developing Western brains for thousands of years. But of course the world is changing and new memes come our way all the time from Asia, and we have contributed a lot to their thought as well.

It is clear that philosophers are not going to surprise biologists with some overlooked item in biologists' worldview. Whether the philosophers concern themselves with environment or genetics or development or behavior, they are dealing with issues that biologists have been trained to think about for a long time. The really good biologists have no difficulty destroying the philosophers' weak foundation for rebuttal.

Face it. People need to study more biology. Then they can make better claims about human nature and, more importantly, reject the bogus claims made by bad biologists!

Here are some specific responses to things you wrote:

PJ: To say that behavior is just the stuff of biology can't be correct.

GG: I agree.

PJ: If biology alone explained all of human behavior, then wouldn't one expect people everywhere to be basically the same since human biology is the same?

GG: No, because environment varies for every living creature.

PJ: If behavior only bubbled upward from biology, and if New Yorkers' and Singaporeans' biology is the same, then one would expect the memes to be the same.

GG: No, this is not correct. In a society that has strict rules governing behavior (like prison sentences for incorrect behavior) it is no surprise to see "correct" behavior. This doesn't mean they don't desire to behave differently, but they are scared. Again, environment (cultural and environmental) plays a crucial role.

PJ: The subway behavior you described exemplifies a rejection of an earlier meme—at one time, New York's subways weren't so disgusting.

GG: Right—when people were afraid to spit or litter because of social rejection. The cultural environment changed and a new behavior emerged (based on the meme of "freedom").

PJ: Here's what makes no sense to me about your position: Let's assume that you're right, that humans are basically highly sophisticated "robots," and they are that way just because that's the way they (are as a result of purely materialistic evolution). Then, logically, it wouldn't make sense for people to want to resist this idea.

GG: This is where you go wrong. The difference between what's logical and what actually happens biologically is what separates the philosopher and the biologist. Most biological phenomena are not logical. That is why theology lost touch with biologists. What is logical about a dinosaur? Or a trilobite? Nothing. William Paley wanted to make nature logical. He is the father of "intelligent design."

***In crossing a heath, suppose I pitched my foot against a stone, and were asked how the stone came to be there, I might possibly answer, that . . . it had lain there forever. . . . But suppose I had found a watch upon the ground, and it should be inquired how the watch happened to be in that place, I should hardly think of the answer which I had before given. . . . For . . . when we come to inspect the watch, we perceive . . . that its several parts are . . . put together for a purpose. . . . We think that the watch must have had a maker.***

**William Paley, theologian and moral philosopher (1806)**

Darwin himself lost interest in Paley's views after he had discovered the implications of natural selection. More recently, Gould beautifully destroyed the notion that biology and evolution are logical. (His book *Wonderful Life* reveals that humans are extremely unlikely creatures; I highly recommend this easy-to-read and interesting book.) He states, "People . . . reject the idea that they are completely predetermined robots." That is because they can't imagine what this means. They have no depth of imagination on the topic because they are totally ignorant about how minds work and what it means to have a complicated brain. It is a very weak argument you advance and I recommend that you abandon it quickly and never use it in a discussion with a neurobiologist. In philosophical circles I am sure it would go over just fine, however.

## MYSTERY

Dear Greg:

I hope your time in California is going well. It seems that the fires are out now. I know well the Waterman Canyon and Del Rosa areas of San Bernardino, part of which went up in flames. Some of my old stomping grounds were decimated.

***Clutching children, pets and belongings, tens of thousands of mountain and foothill residents fled as the billowing monster consumed wildland, homes, and businesses. From its ignition in Waterman Canyon on Saturday, October, 25, 2003, the fiery rampage along the San Bernardino Mountains destroy[ed] 976 homes and result[ed] in six deaths during the crisis. Two months later 14 people were killed as scorched hillsides collapsed during torrential rain, burying parts of Waterman Canyon in over 20 feet of mud and debris.***

**"The Old Fire," rimoftheworld.net**

I did partly misunderstand your note. My impression was that you thought all human behavior was predetermined by internal biological events, so to speak, leaving no room for environment. I see now that that's not right, and I'm glad, as the view I thought you held was pretty reductionistic. (I agree, by the way, that the note I sent you wasn't well thought out—I wrote it after dinner guests overstayed their welcome by about two hours!)

Here are some thoughts and responses to your note.

You seem to concede that there's an element of mystery to human life, though you don't use the word. "Every slight difference adds up to different personalities," you say, and I think you're right—though this needn't be taken as a hard and fast rule. But you also acknowledge that scientists are a long way from being able to pin the stuff of these slight differences down: "In 100 years . . . more will be revealed from neurobiology and behavior." I'm sure you're right about this.

But I'm much more skeptical than you are that what most people see as mystery in life will be completely cleared up. That won't be because people haven't been sufficiently educated but because life really is as people experience it—namely, partly mysterious. I notice that you dedicated your doctoral dissertation to your kids, "the greatest gifts of nature in my life." Perhaps the feelings you have for your children correspond perfectly with the view that these amazingly complex little robots consuming oxygen in a meaningless universe are the products of time + chance, but most people don't see things that way. Maybe it's because they need education.

Or maybe a lot of people would be glad to know as much about neurobiology as they could (I wish I had more time to read about it) because they would find it fascinating; they would find their appreciation for the wondrous complexity of humans bolstered, if not fully explained. I don't know; I don't want to talk nonsense (my recent research involves studies of early-twentieth-century northwestern Alaska!). But I am reluctant to accept the suggestion that neurobiologists are the messiahs of the new age. I'm all for neurobiology but, given the human record, I'm skeptical of people who have the Answer, or who say that they're in the process of arriving at it. We see eye to eye here, though I think that in some ways you're a greater man of faith than I am.

***Don't tell me about the answer***
***'cause then another one will come along soon***
***I don't believe you have the answer***
***I've got ideas too***
***but if you've got enough naiveté***
***and you've got conviction***
***then the answer is perfect for you.***
**Greg Graffin, "The Answer,"** ***Generator*** **(1991)**

If neurobiology is at times fundamentally at odds with common sense and common experience, then life is even more ridiculous than the most committed cynics would have us think.

I wonder if this drive—not for education but for the silver bullet that will finally snuff God—isn't a recent example of what humans have been up to for a long time—really, since the beginning of recorded history. Gilgamesh wanted to take his place among the gods; the builders of the tower at Babel wanted to build an edifice to the heavens; Roman emperors wanted to be gods and snuffed the Christians who refused to play along; the philosophes were certain that they were paving the way to pure rationality; Freud said God is a mental projection; classical behaviorists (not believing in a psyche) said that everything comes down to conditioning (no God, no soul, no mystery).

But now Gilgamesh is an interesting story (people don't base their lives on it), the tower of Babel is a figure of speech, and the Roman emperors are seen as grasping at straws as their empire tottered. The philosophers are seen as influential but also excessively optimistic about human rationalism and, some of them, as highly impractical (claiming, for instance, that human society could be perfected). And Freudianism and strict behaviorism have lost a lot of ground to other psychological theories. In the meantime most educated people—educated, I mean, in a general sense—continue to believe in God. This is an astonishing fact.

Some industrialized cultures have effectively abandoned religion—Sweden, for example, is a very secular country. But I notice that highly secular countries are also countries that require high levels of conformity—I'm thinking of Canada's increasingly repressive speech codes. Guys like us would go crazy in boring, conformist secularist countries like Sweden and Canada.

Think about it: You need God to keep your life interesting. Imagine how bored you'd be if you didn't have religion to be pissed off at. God doesn't mind being of service—that's his job (sort of).

Here's a question: What's a good biological explanation for the amazing success of Christianity? So far as I can tell, no other system of thought (to use a phrase) has succeeded as it has. It has thrived in ancient and postmodern times, in highly industrialized and very simple societies; it lives in democracies and dictatorships, among illiterates and intellectuals, among the poor and the wealthy, and among Africans, Asians, Hispanics, Europeans and Alaska natives. (Last I heard, the largest Christian church in the world is in South Korea.)

The Christian experience ranges from the Pentecostal snake handlers of the Appalachians to the highly ritualistic churches of Eastern Orthodoxy to some of the brainiacs of the Ivy League. The only other system I can think of that seems to have appealed to nearly as wide a range of people (albeit only in the modern world) is communism, which itself could only have been born in a general Christian culture. Judaism is identified with ethnicity; Confucianism, Buddhism and Hinduism haven't caught on in any big way outside Asia; Islam doesn't seem to do well as a minority faith or in democracies.

There must be something about Christianity that makes it especially attractive to humans (understanding that it has many localized and historic competitors). Its tenacity and ability to thrive in radically different circumstances says, at the least, that it holds high appeal.

Peace,
Preston

Dear Preston,

Your last note has a lot of good analysis combined with a thought-provoking point at the end. I have an answer—mostly just more food for thought.

I do not think that neurobiologists are the messiahs of a new age of truth. I don't think there are many neurobiologists (if any) who could give a careful historical account of human affairs that touches on human nature as you do. Human knowledge is created by a collective of workers in all sorts of fields. Neurobiology is one of the newer fields of inquiry. When we add that data to the wealth of data from psychology, evolutionary biology, molecular biology, medicine, etc., we are one step closer to answering the mystery of human life.

What many people fail to appreciate, particularly those not trained in science (although as a historian I know you will appreciate this), is the similarity between an artist's masterwork and the edifice of scientific knowledge. Knowledge accumulates over the generations and it slowly erodes mystery and uncertainty. Often it leads to other mysteries and uncertainties, but not always. The fundamental mysteries of viral and bacterial sepsis, for example, are a thing of the past; smallpox was completely eradicated from the planet, no mystery there. We understand the mechanisms involved in viral and bacterial evolution and infection.

A master painter (or master songwriter) creates a work of art based on collective knowledge from human experiences, past practices, properties of materials and so on. When the work is completed, a source of mystery has been demolished (the complex compulsion that inspired the work), and yet another mystery, or another puzzle, materializes. The artist thinks to himself, "On the next piece I create I shall use a slightly different technique," thereby addressing a different mystery, probably fueled by human curiosity to experiment.

The reason science has been so successful is its precision in solving very useful and life-critical puzzles that stand at the root of human survival. It is far less compromising than art due to its dependence on verifiable knowledge. Science, of course, depends on verification of facts. Art, although it serves to dispel mystery to some degree (an artist's achievements prove that this or that can be accomplished), doesn't stand on a foundation of verifiability. But, curiously, it does depend on accumulated knowledge just like science. Art simply addresses more leisurely mysteries, not those of life and death.

The biological sciences I listed above are concerned with life and death, and they do a better job of explaining most mysteries of humankind better than religion does. That was not always the case of course, but times change and so does humankind's ability to understand life-and-death mysteries.

God is one of the mysteries that has been with us forever, as you point out. Even if neurobiology adds the missing ingredient to psychology and evolutionary biology and behavioral science and allows us to successfully explain God, I am confident there will be other mysteries of human life that will require explanation—more work for the future masters. God is not the end, but a great beginning, a challenge for science to adequately explain. Explaining God is a hurdle for science and, if you ask me, an equal hurdle for theologians.

Which magisterium will be more successful in explaining God to the biologically and psychologically literate? I believe it will be science. Of course, my hope for an educated world is probably a

***Human beings would not even begin to search for something of which they knew nothing or for something which they thought was wholly beyond them. Only the sense that they can arrive at an answer leads them to take the first step. When scientists, following their intuition, set out in search of logical and verifiable explanation of a phenomenon, they are confident . . . that they will find an answer. . . . The same must be equally true of the search for truth when it comes to the ultimate questions. The thirst for truth is so rooted in the human heart that to be obliged to ignore it would cast our existence into jeopardy.***

**Pope John Paul II (1998)**

pipe dream. But if ever I was committed to a cause, it is education.

Your "astonishing fact" about the persistence of Christianity might also be revealed as an eroding mystery. I am not sure that in the most educated countries you find religion on the rise. This would require a good global study. In my travels to Europe, South America, Australia, Japan, Southeast Asia, Mexico and North America I have found that although religion is everywhere, it is far less dominant in the lives of citizens whose countries place high standards on education.

In the most backwater places I have ever visited (remote baracas deep in the Amazon; dirt-road towns in Burma; Jacksonville, Fla.) people had no education, yet religious fetishes were dominant. In the cities where education is highly respected (Tokyo, Berlin, Amsterdam, Stockholm, São Paolo, Sydney, etc.) religious fetishes and churches are rarely encountered.

America, of course, is a hotbed for this kind of analysis. We have very high academic standards for a certain class but very low achievers and low standards in other classes. It would be an important work to map out religious belief in America along class lines. My prediction: Education indeed plays a role in religious belief; the more educated would show a lower ranking along several variables for religious belief.

---

***The Harris survey reports that 79% of Americans believe in a deity, and that 66% were "absolutely certain" this to be true. Atheists, those who "do not believe in a God," accounted for 9% of respondents, while 12% may fall into the category of "not sure." . . . Even with the high rate of god belief, though, Harris found that only 55% of Americans attend a religious service "a few times a year," with only 36% attending once a month or more often. Twenty-six percent claimed to attend a house of worship every week. . . . Most countries in Europe have a significantly lower rate of religious observance. Many including Norway, Denmark, Sweden and even Russia have rates under 20%. . . . Education [seems] to have a modest role in whether one [is] atheist or theist. Eighty-two percent of those with a high school education or less reported that they believed in a god. That figure dropped with "some college" (77%), "college" (78%) and "post graduate (73%).***

**Conrad F. Goeringer, *American Atheist Newsletter* (2003)**

---

As for the success of Christianity, there is an explanation of it in my Ph.D. dissertation. It is a quote by Richard Dawkins that describes how a child's brain might be "wired" to "believe what your parents tell you." That is a simple mechanism that not only explains why Christianity is so popular in our Christian society, but also why atheism tends to run in the family. If a child is never exposed to concepts of God, she still wonders about things. Science answers a lot of her questions without reference to any intelligent designer.

What makes Christianity attractive? Well, during the Middle Ages there were very strong motives for loving Christianity. The symbolism of burning a human being alive on a stake in the center of town passes down through the generations to create a powerful reminder of what might happen if you are seen as a "heretic." I worry, even today, about persecution for my beliefs. It would perhaps be easier for me to conform to an active Christian lifestyle. I am privileged to live in this time in history and in a supportive familial and social atmosphere where I can express my ideas without too much fear. But plenty of people don't have that privilege and for them every indicator points toward believing in a Christian God. So I guess it is because of fear that Christianity is so popular. Fear is not always recognized by the self.

Some happy Christians are totally unaware of their own daily trepidation. It is only the most intelligent people I have met who are forthright about expressing their fears and who understand how fear might affect their motives and beliefs. My fear of persecution for my beliefs is not as powerful as my fear of failure at accomplishment. So the best way for me to achieve is to make music that questions religion, pursue scientific academic avenues, and pass along goodness to my children. It seems productive.

I have been asked to give a talk at the Cornell Christian Faculty Fellowship. It seems that you are not the only religious academic who is interested in hearing about the views of the evolutionists. I welcome the invitation. I expect a lively discussion.

Sincerely,
Greg

P.S. Please tell me how *Brideshead Revisited* is supposed to initiate a sense of compassion toward religious people. I saw the story as depicting religion as a horrific burden on the happiness of Brideshead family, all the way up to the end of the story in the eventual dissolution of Charles's relationship.

It just dawned on me yesterday, during songwriting, that I had deleted that message you sent a while back that asked me about *Brideshead Revisited* (remember—because I hadn't yet finished the story).

---

Dear Greg:

I've been nailed by the Tidal Wave: midterms, students in revolt because I hammered the bad grammar in their papers, writing deadlines, the lecture I mentioned before to finish (delivered it last night in Dallas). Ever have so much going on that you get panicky? That was me up to yesterday—and my parents, from San Bernardino, have just arrived for the weekend! So let me catch my breath and digest your last letter.

I heard the California fire was heading for San Fernando . . . ?

Peace,
Preston

---

Dear Preston,

I am going to LA on Monday. My mom, who lives in the S.F. Valley, said the smoke was awful but it has been contained.

The talk today at Cornell Christian Faculty Fellowship went

well. The largest complaint was that my definition of theism is misleading. Apparently I wasn't kind enough to God. I guess I said a theist's God is one that manipulates and intervenes and this was offensive to one of the audience members.

In the pre-talk prayer, the emcee said thank you to God "and we hope you will speak through Greg today to help enlighten us." Apparently I am not totally due all the credit for the ideas in my work!

They also criticized my "null hypothesis"—that since God can't be found scientifically, any reason to believe in God is nullified. I'm not sure what the problem is. It seems simple to me. Can you explain something better using God than using natural science? Have a good day.

Sincerely,
Greg

---

Dear Greg:

All the best to you as you return to the land of the Apocalypse. Mudslides soon to follow. I have saved our correspondence, going back to the first note. You'd probably be amazed at the thick stack that's grown. Everyone's gone to the store, so I have some quiet time to work with.

I'm listening to Handel's *Messiah* right now—one of the great Christian works, written by a person who was, at best, nominally religious. That reminds me that an atheist punk singer has spurred me to think more about Christianity than any preacher I've heard. Ain't life strange? That's something you can ask the Cornell Christian Faculty Fellowship: Why do American churches mimic the general culture—brainlessness and emotionalism on one hand, a mildly Christianized political correctness on the other?

Now to *Brideshead*. Your question—how is *Brideshead Revisited* supposed to initiate a sense of compassion for religious people?—is a good one. And in a way I suppose it answers itself. Jesus and St. Paul (the latter wrote most of the New Testament) said repeatedly that the normal status of the Christian is to be scorned, persecuted, held in contempt, pitied and so on. "Woe unto you if the world loves you," says Jesus.

Their point is that, as a matter of course, being a Christian means precisely *not* eliciting the compassion of others. Instead, expect persecution and scorn. This is the norm for Christians in much of the world—e.g., China, Pakistan and the Sudan. But "here in the land of the free time" (to quote you), Christians think they should run everything—and they're just as fat, unhealthy and ignorant as everyone else. "Christianity" is a cultural commodity.

Yesterday I told my students that America's Christians

***We justified the world, and condemned as heretics those who tried to follow Christ. The result was a nation that became Christian . . . but at the cost of true discipleship. . . . Our humanitarian sentiment made us give that which was holy to the scornful and unbelieving. We poured forth unending streams of grace. But the call to follow Jesus in the narrow way was hardly ever heard.***

**Dietrich Bonhoeffer, theologian killed by Nazis (1937)**

could effect a revolution immediately if every one of them chucked their TVs in the garbage. But the Christians are just as addicted to brainless entertainment, and just as afraid of silence, as everyone else. There will be no revolution. The Sudanese Christians get snuffed and sold into slavery, but they're just Africans.

In *Brideshead Revisited*, who is the one seemingly genuine Christian from beginning to end? Cordelia. And though she's goofy, she's endearing and is, as they say, the real deal. She gives her life in service to others. She likes the agnostic, Charles Ryder; she doesn't find him threatening; she loves Sebastian, despite his self-destructiveness; she's always hopeful.

***"Poor Sebastian! . . . It's too pitiful. How will it end?"***

***"I think I can tell you exactly how, Charles. I've seen others like him, and I believe they are very near and dear to God. He'll live on, half in, half out of, the community, a familiar figure pottering round with his broom and his bunch of keys. He'll be a great favourite with the old fathers. . . . Everyone will know about his drinking. . . . Then one morning, after one of his drinking bouts, he'll be picked up at the gate dying, and show by a mere flicker of the eyelid that he is conscious when they give him the last sacraments. It's not such a bad way of getting through one's life."***

**Evelyn Waugh, *Brideshead Revisited*, 1951**

The miserable people are those who resist God in one way or another (with the possible exception of Bridey, who's just pompous but also, in a way, endearing). The mother can't rely on God's grace—she wants to micromanage everything. Sebastian remains a believer who at the same time wants to fight God, and God lets him take his own course while never letting him go. (Cordelia says that maybe Sebastian is fortunate in that in his last days, he will provide monks with an occasion to serve a seemingly wasted life.) Julia denies her faith—lives as if it's false—but can't really shake free of it. Charles is the "agnostic" around whose ankle God has a rope. With a "twitch on the thread" God will bring Charles around. It will feel like a painful yank at the time. But as Charles reflects in the chapel at the end of the story, he sees the freedom he has found—the last line of the movie and the book has a soldier saying to Charles, "You're looking unusually cheerful today."

But what of Julia and Charles's breakup? Is that cruel of God to require? Charles doesn't think so. He says to Julia, "I hope your heart may break; but I do understand." If he really loves Julia—before this time does Charles really love anything?—then he couldn't ask her to set up, in Julia's words, "a rival good to God's."

Charles demonstrates his love for Julia by recognizing that he can't ask her to give up the most important thing in her life. Maybe there's another way, but Julia doesn't see it: "The worse I am, the more I need God. I can't shut myself out from his mercy. That is what it would mean," she says to Charles, "starting a life with you, without him." Charles, we know, finds (for the first time) a sense of peace after the breakup. Of Julia we have no word. But the book's really about Charles.

There's that famous quote from Vietnam—"To save

the village we had to destroy it." For obvious reasons, the quote is ludicrous. And yet it conveys something true about life. Muscles are built up only after being broken down. Marathoners succeed only after miles of sweat. Great punk bands are built on the foundations of unpleasant experiences (the famous—infamous?—second album). As you say, "Our evolution didn't hinge on passivity."

I have a student who thinks highly of her writing ability. She is an English major—ergo, she must be a great writer! Yes, she has some talent, but her writing needs a

***INQUIRY BOX***

**Evelyn Waugh wrote that the theme of Brideshead Revisited is "the operation of divine grace on a group of diverse but closely connected characters." The theological meaning of the word grace, which comes from the Latin *gratia,* is difficult to pin down, but usually it refers to God's giving of mercy, kindness and compassion to people who don't deserve it—which, Christians think, includes everyone. Christians believe that God's grace is available to everyone, but is extended most fully to those who willingly accept it. Sometimes God will "help" people to accept his grace by allowing them to make messes of their lives, at which point they might become willing to let God into their lives. It seems that, in various ways, this is what happens to the characters in *Brideshead Revisited.***

**Greg's response is that, in the novel, Christianity just makes people miserable. Preston agrees that characters in the novel are miserable, but thinks that this misery leads to a kind of freedom.**

**If you have read the novel, or seen the BBC film production, do you think the characters' misery leads to anything worthwhile? If they experience anything worthwhile, could what they experience be called "grace"?**

**If you haven't read the novel or seen the BBC production, do so and see what you think.**

lot of work, and she is quite unhappy with me for refusing to agree with her lofty self-assessment. Apparently I'm tougher on her writing than her other professors.

Because I care about her as a student, and because I care about writing, I will continue to press her. She will continue to not like it and, perhaps, to wave other ambitious students away from my classes. But I hope that in time she will see the good thing I'm doing. For her to become a really good writer, her current belief needs to be challenged. She'll be the better for it.

This is something like what happened to Charles and Julia. They had to give up beliefs about what they thought was good for something that was really better. This sort of process usually involves unpleasantness. Life is a learning process, then we die.

Now that the smoke has cleared, your dissertation goes to the top of the pile, along with about eight books to review. Thanks for sending it.

Peace,
Preston

## FAN MAIL

Dear Preston,

I usually don't do this (forward fan mail) but this letter is such an interesting parallel with our earlier correspondence that I thought you might appreciate reading it. This letter is one that I read this week. It is very typical of a lot of the mail Bad Religion receives. It reveals that "born-agains," probably the group most responsible for America's unusually high statistic for religiosity, are numerous and not very liberal with their children when it comes to faith. It is a sad statement. We hardly ever receive letters like this from other countries (and foreign mail makes up about 30% of our fan mail).

Sincerely,
Greg

*Dear Mr. Graffin,*

*I just wanted to write you a letter explaining to you how much your music has really helped me. I've listened to you guys for about two years now and I never really understood your lyrics until about five months ago. When I met my current boyfriend, he asked what one of my favorite bands was and I told him Bad Religion. Well it turns out you're one of his favorites also. He told me a lot about you guys. I just listened to the music and never really got behind it, focusing on how your music deals with disbelief in faith, the government and other things.*

*Since I entered high school I have really taken a look at my religious beliefs because there was more attention drawn to it since high school kids are "more mature" and talked about deeper things. In middle school nobody ever talked about religion.*

*In my stupid attempt to become popular I started going to Young Life (it's like a Christian youth club) my sophomore year. I went so I could meet all the "cool kids" because they went. After about two months of Young Life I realized most of the kids who went were also the kids who got drunk and high on the weekend. Then they came and put on their "good religious kid" facade in an attempt to make it seem that Young Life had a real effect on them.*

*Half of the kids who go to Young Life go for the social time. I was guilty of that too because I thought I could meet the right people that way. I considered stopping going because I felt so fake but my boyfriend at the time went, and he was popular, so I figured I should still go.*

*The one time that I finally realized I had no definite beliefs was at Young Life. The leader was talking about a wedding where Jesus came and did something to the food and wine so it never ran out, which makes no sense at all! He was saying that Jesus had the capability to defy the laws of physics and everything else.*

***When the wine was gone, Jesus' mother said to him, "They have no more wine."***

***"Dear woman, why do you involve me?" Jesus replied. "My time has not yet come."***

***His mother said to the servants, "Do whatever he tells you."***

***Nearby stood six stone water jars . . . each holding from twenty to thirty gallons.***

***Jesus said to the servants, "Fill the jars with water"; so they filled them to the brim.***

***Then he told them, "Now draw some out and take it to the master of the banquet."***

***They did so, and the master of the banquet tasted the water that had been turned into wine.***

**John 2:3-9**

*After hearing this story I had a hard time deciding what I believed. I think I continued to "believe" in God and everything else because it's the norm and I didn't want to be ostracized.*

*My mom forced me to go to church with her. In church I never listened and even if I did, I never believed any of it. I don't understand how people can have such faith in things they've never seen before, and preach about faith and pleasing God. After a while of thinking about what "beliefs" I had, I realized I don't really have any.*

*I also looked at evolution. It's impossible to look at monkeys and not see the connection from one species to another. My junior year my mom said something to me about biology and evolution, so I told her I believed in evolution and she looked at me like, "How can you believe such crap?"*

*I've still never explained all of my so-called "beliefs" to my mom. She tells me to pray when things get rough. I just say, "Yeah, OK," then roll my eyes when I'm out of sight. As a born-again Christian, she has no tolerance for disbelief or disrespect to God or anything.*

*One day I asked her how she can believe in stories like the wine at the wedding, and she said you just have to have faith. My faith is in science and nature and coincidence. My best friend even gets mad when I say I don't have any beliefs about anything. She told me one time that I'm intentionally trying to be a nonconformist. Needless to say, that brought about one of our rare fights. I never came out with my opposition to religion until this year.*

*Once I started to read your lyrics, I saw that you struggle with your beliefs too. I don't have any friends who are going with me on this move toward religious nonaffiliation, so your music really helped me understand that there are more people who feel this way. The fact that you are public with your feelings on religion gave me an extra push to be public with mine.*

*This year at school I decided to not say the Pledge of Alle-*

*giance because it refers to God. I feel like I'm empathizing with other kids who don't believe in God. If I were Muslim or Buddhist, I wouldn't say the pledge because my beliefs would be based on some other religion.*

*In English class this year we had to write an essay on a famous person we would like to have lunch with, why, and what we would talk about with that person. Before the essay was written, our teacher read our choices aloud and asked us who the people were and what we would talk about with them. I chose to write my essay on you, and I said that I would like to talk about breaking free of religion.*

*When I expressed my disbelief in God the teacher and a couple students gave me looks like, "She's going to hell now." That experience made me tell my story even more. There is one really "godly" girl in that class, with the WWJD pins and s*** all over her clothes and she doesn't talk to me anymore. I'm glad, actually, because I'd prefer to not hear her preach to me.*

*My mom and aunt preach to me, and that's when my mom and I fight a lot because I tell her I don't want to hear it.*

*In government class we had to state something we strongly opposed; I said belief in religion. Only one kid agreed with me. Another kid after me said he strongly believed in God and opposed people who didn't. It just shows how ignorant he was to not accept my beliefs. The kid who does believe in God also goes to Young Life.*

*In school I get really pissed off when teachers talk about religion or make references to the Bible. Because of your music and my connection to your lyrics I'm more confident about my view on religion and I express my views when I need to.*

*Right now my mission is to collect all of your CDs so I can get even more of what I crave—something to connect with. So thanks again for having the guts to tell everyone your beliefs and not care what they say.*

*Sincerely,*

*Jenny*

*P.S. When are you guys going on tour again, and if you are, do you plan on coming to southern Virginia? I would really love to see you guys.*

---

Dear Greg:

Thanks for passing Jenny's note to me. I identify very much with what she wrote. I have been discouraged lately with many of my students who in some ways sound like the kids she knows. They are good with outward piety; they know the Jesus lingo. But their "faith" seems to make no practical difference in their lives. Perhaps by making them smug, it makes them worse people than they might be otherwise.

---

***Love the Lord your God with all your heart and with all your soul and with all your mind and with all your strength.***

**Mark 12:30**

---

Jesus said that people should love God with their minds as well as their souls. I think he said that because he knows how few people—of any persuasion—really want to use their minds. So he says that people honor

God by using the brains God gave them. Most of the genuinely intelligent and thoughtful people I know are Christians. But Jenny is right to suggest that many Christians act and speak brainlessly. I don't think it's because they're Christians; it's because they're people. But it's a disgrace when Christians are "average" in this way.

Before returning to university teaching, I taught for three years at a Christian prep school—one of the old-fashioned kinds that teaches Latin and occasionally Greek, along with other great stuff. I think Jenny would be amazed at the intellectual horsepower at that Christian school.

St. James says that people who presume to be teachers among Christians are taking on a very serious task.

***Not many of you should presume to be teachers . . . because you know that we who teach will be judged more strictly.***

**James 3:1**

It sounds to me like the guy who shot off his mouth about Jesus, physics and wine blew it. Does he have inside information? And anyway, while a literal, unimaginative reading of that story is fine, if that's as far as it goes, a lot of potentially interesting questions are left unanswered. Why did Jesus perform his first miracle at a party? Why does it seem that Jesus is playing mind games with his mom? Why doesn't his mom do what he asks—namely, to quit bugging him? But mediocre minds don't like contemplation, so they concoct pseudointellectual trash. I know exactly the kind of meeting Jenny has described. I hated them by the time I was 16, and I don't go to them now. I guess I always had the advantage of being individualistic.

I think that the answer Jenny's mom gave to her—"You just have to have faith"—is partly true and partly false. First, I would say that her mom is probably doing the best she can with what she has, so an amount of genuine tolerance (as opposed to the cheap PC kind) may be in order.

But much in life does depend on faith. I have faith, for example, that these symbols I'm putting together in the form of a note will make sense to whoever reads it. In a way, this takes a lot of faith. This is the first time in the history of the world that this exact note is being written. It's a new thing. But I trust that you and Jenny will be able to understand it. That's a kind of faith.

But the important point is that it's a reasonable faith. And this is where people go wrong with ideas about blind faith. I keep looking for the passage where Jesus tells people to exercise blind faith. He never does. I think people take the blind faith route because it's easy; it requires no intellectual work. And for some people—perhaps especially for people whose minds have been numbed by TV—that works. But it isn't the Christian ideal. It would be hard to paint St. Paul, or Augustine, or Aquinas, or Pascal, or Kierkegaard, or Dietrich Bonhoeffer as intellectual lightweights.

The sad part is that the whole thing about the Christian club being a popularity hangout is antithetical to

***Belief is a wise wager. Granted that faith cannot be proved, what harm will come to you if you gamble on its truth and it proves false? If you gain, you gain all; if you lose, you lose nothing. Wager, then, without hesitation, that He exists.***

**Blaise Pascal, mathematician and philosopher (1669)**

everything Jesus said. It would make no sense to the great majority of Christians around the world. It would make no sense to Christians in secular parts of this country (such as in Sonoma County, California), where serious Christians are a small minority. Never does Jesus say that hanging out with him will make a person popular; in fact, he quite explicitly says the opposite. The Bible Belt gets this exactly wrong.

Instead of being put off, I wonder if a better option for Jenny wouldn't be to commit herself to show the phonies what the real thing is like. She can tutor kids on the poor side of town as a service to God (and because it's a good thing to do); she can read philosophy and science as a service to God (and because it'll make her smarter); she can give away a portion of the money she earns to a good charity as a service to God (and because people need help); she can ask her teachers tough questions as a service to God (and because many teachers have no business being in the classroom).

She can tell God that she wants to know if it's reasonable to take him seriously, and if so, then it's partly his job to make that clear.

And she needs to do her part. God doesn't mind

doubt—it often leads to liberation and a faith worth something. It did for me.

---

***Da mihi, Domine, scire et intelligere, utrum sit prius invocare te an laudare te, et scire te prius sit an invocare te.***

***"Help me, Lord, to discern and to understand whether it is better first to call upon you or to praise you, or whether it is better first to know you before calling upon you."***

**St. Augustine, church father, *Confessions* (A.D. 397)**

---

I'd like to have Jenny as a university student. I know many of my colleagues would as well.

Peace,
Preston

---

*The next day Preston edited the above note and sent it to Jenny. She responded.*

*Dear Preston,*

*Thanks for reading my letter and taking the time to reply to it. Now it may not sound like I am trying to be open-minded, but I really am. I just don't understand a lot of things and it's hard for me to grasp some of the ideas you propose. I guess I am one of those people who have to physically see something to believe it. I don't even know. Maybe the one thing that made me start questioning my beliefs was Young Life. I know that most of the kids who attend are totally going against what its purpose is, but even when I did go to Young Life and listened, some of the lessons made no sense to me.*

*I see what you mean about having faith, and I do have reasonable faith, but religious faith is what I lack. Since you said you looked through the Bible for the passage on blind faith and couldn't find one, it makes me wonder where the idea came from. To me it seems like a concept people are making up to explain why things occur the way they do and how.*

*For me religious faith is hard to comprehend because it's requesting that I have faith in something I can't see, touch or have proof even exists. I can understand a belief in Jesus because he was a real person and history can prove that. But what about God? Who is God? What does he look like? Where is he?*

*Before I started to question my beliefs, God was a "spirit" to me, a nonexistent being that I occasionally made requests of. But then I realized I'm praying to nothing, just some society-approved "person." If I prayed to a tree people might wonder what drugs I was taking, or if I was out of my mind. For all anybody knows, God could be some fictional character that people made up a long time ago to explain unknown phenomena.*

*I haven't read much about the creation of the universe, but to my understanding there are two theories: the big bang theory and God created it. From what I do know of the big bang theory, the earth and everyone on it could have started on their own, without any outside help due to evolution and how nature works. So where does God come in on that?*

*In dealing with the few other people I know with no faith, some had traumatic experiences with loved ones that spurred their disbelief. My family has a long history of health problems. My grandma had two strokes in a week, a different grandma came down with ovarian cancer and died, then my step mom got cancer for a second time. The uncle I was closest to died about a month ago from angiosarcoma of the liver, a very rare form of cancer. So my question is, Why these people?*

*I realize that everyone dies and that there are "sacrifices" (I don't want that to sound like the wrong kind of sacrifice, not like an animal-ritual sacrifice or anything!), and without these deaths, many other things may not occur. But if Jesus and God wanted there to be peace in the world, and God created everything, then why did he make such destructive diseases?*

*Another topic is heaven and hell. When I was a child, I went to church until my parents got divorced. Later we started going again. When I was eight years old my mom and I were really, really poor and she looked to church for refuge. They gave us food and that gave my mom a basis for reestablishing her beliefs. As a kid I never really understood what went on in church, I just regurgitated the information that was given to me. After we got back on our feet we again stopped going to church.*

*I vaguely remember a few stories from the Bible, but when I was little I never cared, so I didn't listen. But I do know about heaven and hell. My step mom is a devout Catholic and I am forced to attend church with her when I'm with my dad, but even as I listen to the priest preaching about doing good deeds so you can go to heaven, I am bewildered. The serious Christian's goal is to get to heaven. But what is heaven? To me when you die, you die; you don't go anyplace. Christians teach of the soul ascending to heaven or descending to hell, but is there proof of such a physical place? Some Christians may say you have to have faith that there are such places.*

*I will point out that I am a hypocrite in one way. In the case of my Uncle Ron—the one who just passed away—I like to pretend he is in heaven, even though I don't know if I believe in it. But if there were such a place, I know he would be there. When he died I wondered what would happen. His body would lie in its crypt in the ground, but to many his "soul" would go to heaven to one day be joined by his family. To me that's saying that heaven is a place where dead people hang out. But that's impossible.*

*In your letter you said that some Christians say brainless things. Well everyone says brainless things. If you label one group you should label them all. I don't think Christians are any smarter than non-Christians; therefore, I don't believe non-Christians are any smarter than believers. It's just a matter of genetics and self-motivation.*

*I'm not pissed off at the phonies, they just annoy me. I get pissed off at people who try to force their beliefs on me to try to "help" me. The only person who can help me is myself. Growing up without a strong background in religion and faith is, I think, the main reason I question God and everything that deals with him. I do plan on reading some philosophy and science to help me better understand everything, but not as a service to God. I need to build concrete beliefs for myself before I can decide whether I want to believe in God or not.*

*The conformist in me says, "Yes, believe in God; it's what's right." But the other part of me says, "Question religion and don't believe anything you can't accept." I don't consider myself an atheist. Maybe that's because I'm still only 17 and trying to figure out who and what I am. But deciphering my beliefs will be like trying to read some incomprehensible language.*

*Sincerely,*

*Jenny*

Dear Jenny:

I just got your note and haven't had time to read it carefully—I have two papers to grade and then must run to class. I'll read it as soon as I get back to my office.

One thing I want you to know right now is that this afternoon I read your letter to Greg (without giving away personal info about you) to my class of forty-six university students. I'm going to do the same thing in my next class of twenty students. Your letter makes excellent points that Christians need to consider. The class was supposed to talk about the First World War, but we ended up talking about your letter instead. Thanks for making the class probably the best one we've had all semester. I think the next class I have today will be even more interested—it's an honors class full of bright students.

God bless,
Preston

---

*Jenny and Preston carried on their own correspondence. Mostly they just swapped stories about life. Jenny wrote about working at Pizza Hut, getting ready for Advanced Placement exams, her freshman year as a psychology major at a university in Missouri, and her sophomore year at a college back in Virginia. In the late summer of 2004 she saw Bad Religion in concert. "The show was great!" she wrote. "I was really close to the front. Greg did talk a lot; I was surprised—I figured they would just sing and say a few words, but they were really funny. The bass player messed up, so they all laughed and started the song over again. Then Greg started on the second verse instead of the first. Then he messed up again, and then they got it right. They were great in concert."*

## CHRISTIANITY AND VIOLENCE

Dear Greg:

I'm reading your Ph.D. dissertation and enjoying it immensely. Aside from being informative, it's a good read. And depending on who's speaking, the interviews are thought-provoking, interesting and entertaining.

***Believing that there is not a god, you have as little evidence for that as you do for believing there is a god. You have no evidence for either. . . . You can't answer the questions except by an act of faith, and if it's an act of faith, it's just as much as act of faith as saying there's no god as saying there is a god.***

**John M. Thoday, geneticist (2003)**

But Richard Dawkins coughs up some very deep nonsense. I think he should stick to evolutionary biology. He clearly has no idea what he's talking about when it comes to "canonical religion." And his bit about children just accepting what their parents tell them is junk. There's a very real difference between a child recognizing that it's not wise to swim with crocodiles (to use his example) and a child just accepting, and continuing to accept, what his parents say about God.

I have no difficulty bringing to mind Christians I know who grew up in irreligious homes, or in thinking of people who grew up in religious homes but have left the family's faith. You yourself get letters from kids who are in the process of rejecting their parents' views.

***Perhaps, child brains are shaped by genetic natural selection to follow a rule of thumb that says believe whatever your parents tell you. . . . The world is a dangerous place. . . . It's too dangerous to discover by trial and error. Like, "don't swim in the river because there are crocodiles." You just have to believe what your parents tell you. If Darwinian selection has programmed your child to believe whatever your parents tell you, then [that leads to acceptance of the belief] that you have to sacrifice a goat to the "Great Juju" in the sky.***

**Richard Dawkins, evolutionary biologist (2003)**

My wife and I tell our 19-month-old daughter not to eat cat food. She knows it's naughty to do so—that's why she shuts the door to the room the cat food's in. But she still eats it! And how does "teen rebellion" fit in? Maybe Dawkins meant something more complicated than what he appears to say—i.e., "Kids buy what their parents say; that explains the persistence of religion." But as it stands, it's just flat-out bogus. It doesn't fit with common experience.

You grew up in an irreligious home. But among other things, your dissertation is part of a religious quest. You want to know the answer to the questions, What does the high priesthood of the metaphysical naturalist school think? What's orthodox for them and what's not?

On another topic: I want to challenge something implied in a few of your notes, namely, that Christianity has been a source (in the West) of unparalleled oppression and violence and that if Christians had their way, they'd subjugate everyone. This is a popular view and, like most popular views, it's mostly false. Secularist ideologies have led to much more hardship, political oppression, economic chaos and mass killing than any Western theological system has.

Let me say at the outset that there's no point in trying to "explain away" the violence that has been, and still is, perpetrated in Christ's name. Self-defense is one thing and just war theory is generally accepted, but torching people because they don't accept a certain theological point of view can't be defended from the New Testament.

But history is complicated, and no responsible historian I know of claims that theology was the only motivator behind the witch trials and various inquisitions. Instead they point to tensions and uncertainties created by the usual suspects: political challenges (nobles versus lords, lords versus princes, princes versus emperors, emperors versus the pope), economic change, devastating disease, bad weather and the need to explain the origins of these problems. It's universally accepted (except among some teachers who imbibe their knowledge from TV docudramas) that the exceedingly brutal "wars of religion" had much less to do with religion than they did with political power and the desire of unleashed young men to rape and pillage. (Ditto for the conquistadors in the New World.)

Also, very few people were executed for religious reasons without trial. Of course, the evidence gathered at the trials was usually bogus. (At Salem, George Burroughs was found guilty of being a warlock partly because he had an unusually large number of toads living on his property!) But trials were conducted, and a lot of people were set free. At Salem over 100 people were accused; about 20 were executed. Once the hysteria subsided, the authorities acknowledged publicly that those executed were innocent, and money was given to their families. This is all quite pathetic, but the image one has of Puritans out to fry all disbelievers is false. The famous "heretics" Anne Hutchinson and Roger Williams were not executed.

If in the Middle Ages the big boys in the church were out to snuff the theologically impure, they did a crappy job of it. It's generally recognized now that theological orthodoxy was probably in short supply among "common" people in much of Europe, which was overwhelmingly rural. Old pagan beliefs were mixed with Christian ones. Thus the current celebrations of Christmas and Easter, holidays ("holy days") that contain both Christian and pagan elements.

Europe began to become a more humane place at precisely the time literacy was spreading, partly as a result of the Protestant Reformation. The more people could read the New Testament for themselves, the more they—or at least some—could see that Jesus never asked his disciples to toast the hard-hearted.

But even if the inaccurate clichés about Christian violence were correct, systematic mass slaughter without trial has been an innovation (since the advent of Christ) of secularists. We see it first with the mass killing by drowning *(les noyades)* of the anti-Christian fanatics of the French Revolution. We see it in Stalin's atheistic regime. In Hitler's anti-Jewish, anti-Christian regime. And then we see it in other places where secularist ideology was imported—Mao's China, Pol Pot's Cambodia.

And today existential misery and suicide are highest precisely in the places where secularism is most prevalent—the example I know best is Quebec. Forty-five years ago Quebecers had a strong Catholic identity; now the churches are empty, nationalism hasn't proved itself a satisfying religion and societal malaise there is profound.

***The Province of Quebec has one of the highest suicide rates in North America, with approximately 1500 cases per year. It constitutes the principal cause of death amongst males under 40 years of age.***

**Quebec Mental Health Neuroscience Network (2005)**

Peace,
Preston

---

Dear Preston,

I intend to answer your letter; however, it is absolute crunch time right now. High pressure. These are the last remaining days of songwriting before we enter the studio and never has there been greater pressure on the quality of the songs. I have a hard time focusing on other things when I am in a songwriting phase.

Sincerely,
Greg

*At this time Greg became completely focused on writing the songs for* The Empire Strikes First *and then on recording them. A couple weeks after recording was completed, he went to Europe to promote Bad Religion's new CD. BR's 2004 North American tour soon followed. The band returned to Europe in the summer of 2005.*

*Around the same time, Preston began work on two books (beside this one) and had to put a lot of time into preparing courses he would be teaching for the first time. His wife was also eager for him to stay away from the computer after he had come home from work.*

*The following notes were written after BR's 2004 tour.*

## PROXIMATE VERSUS ULTIMATE MEANING

Dear Preston,

Perhaps you have seen the song "All There Is" on the new Bad Religion disc. Every night when I sing that song on stage I feel like the people in the audience hear the words but never really internalize the implications of the rhetorical question, "Can that be all there is?"

***In my rectory of doubt***
***I kneel to pray like one devout***
***as time the great gray dreamless sleep***
***of a useless modern God***
***erodes away each storied day***
***as wretched Adams***
***with hell to pay***
***content upon a rail of pain, for just a little rain***

**Greg Graffin, "All There Is," *The Empire Strikes First* (2004)**

It seems that most people want to believe there is more meaning in the universe than actually exists. There is a strong emotional drive to find meaning, which might be "hard-wired" in our brains or a cultural universal found in all human societies perhaps. This drive leads many people to accept religion readily because theologies reassure us that indeed there is an ultimate meaning and an ultimate purpose to human life.

I never accepted such myths, probably because I was surrounded by skeptics in my upbringing. Yet still I believed that I led a meaningful life and that I mattered in some way. As I grew up I realized that I mattered a lot less than I thought. By this I mean only that as I grew more worldly and empathetic I learned that there is a world out there that exists and functions regardless of my presence and influence. To me, this is a part of growth and maturation, a humility that develops with age and experience.

Part of the process of growing and maturing requires the rewriting of previous worldviews. Consider the meaning of Christmas to a young American kid. It's basically a time when a wonderful man comes to your house one night every year and leaves a bunch of presents. Soon, a child learns that there is no Santa Claus; it's the parents who buy the gifts and lovingly wrap them and put them under the tree. The meaning of Christmas and even the purpose of Christmas changes as the kid grows. After the reality sinks in, the kid rewrites the tradition, or rather his mind rewrites it for him, because the holiday is so much fun and so meaningful to the family that he need not let this reality—there's no Santa!—ruin the proximal meaning of Christmas. In short, it doesn't matter that Santa Claus isn't real; the meaning of Christmas has tons of proximate meaning.

I think there are all sorts of realities that we learn as we mature, and we are forced to rewrite our worldviews. I was never taught any of the traditional religious worldviews. That is the reason the world began to make sense for me rather late in life, during my studies of natural history at university. The world became more meaningful to me as I learned about the fragility and complexity of our ecological communities and geological processes. I felt like I was a part of a great biological tradition and I felt lucky to be able to witness the "grandeur of life" with a deep appreciation for its intricacy and knowledge about its functioning. The deep sense of satisfaction I got, and still get, from studying and participating in nature, leaves me perfectly content with the proximate meaning of it all.

Even though I can't formulate any ultimate meaning for it all—I know I am just a small part of it and I will soon be dead and so will my offspring—I know that the studying, teaching and sharing of natural history provides a lifetime of meaningful enterprise for me. I don't feel empty or at any kind of loss from my conclusion that life has no ultimate purpose. Passing on proximately meaningful traditions and rituals is enough for me. It always has felt like enough for me. Maybe that will change, but I doubt it. As I have learned more I have felt an even greater pull toward my conclusion that there are no ultimates.

The so-called "existence" of notions that there is more than this world alone I whole-heartedly reject. It might be that we are taught poorly as kids. It might be a symptom of our imperfect education that we are told there is an ultimate meaning to things. What if our society stopped passing along inaccuracies by removing such language from the learning curriculum? Would the notion of ultimate purpose cease to exist? I believe strongly that it would be virtually nonexistent in society. We can live with proximate purpose alone and still live fully satisfied lives without the mythology of ultimates. I believe humans would feel just as emotional and loving and caring in the absence of ultimates as they do going about carelessly thinking that a better world awaits them when they die. I think that we, like other social organisms, use proximate meaning and proximate purpose to get through life. Ultimates are an invention of theology, and one we cannot easily shake from our culture.

You have said to me that you don't even know what ultimate meaning could be. *[Greg is referring to a note of Preston's that has been lost.]* Almost everyone believes their life has ultimate meaning, especially religiously minded people. This comes from the belief that God somehow pre-ordained their conception and loves them specially—from their belief that they are living for God and because of God. God caused them to be born. God is the reason for everything. Since you are educated it is no wonder you find it hard to understand what ultimate meaning could be. You learned theology, you are highly literate, and I know you read about science. Your struggle is maintaining a belief in ultimate meaning in the face of learning more and more about a world whose natural phenomena stare you right in the face and say: There are no ultimates, my friend, when it comes to meaning and purpose.

Sincerely,
Greg

---

Dear Greg:

Of the inspiring passages in your note, the one I most identify with is this one: "As I grew more worldly and empathetic I learned that there is a world out there that exists and functions regardless of my presence and influence. To me, this is a part of growth and maturation, a humility that develops with age and experience."

I also have learned that there are great limits to what I can accomplish and that, for the most part, it doesn't matter what I do. I don't mean that it's irrelevant whether I'm a thief or a nurse. But so long as I'm not intentionally harming other people, it doesn't really matter in the big scheme of themes whether I teach or write or clean floors. Whatever I do is unlikely to endure for long on earth, so I should focus on using whatever gifts I have, on doing what I like to do and doing it well.

Fortunately for me, I've found a way to get paid for doing what I like. Most people aren't so fortunate. The obvious fact that the vast majority of people and their actions slip into oblivion soon after their death has been commented on from ancient times. It's at the heart of the "human condition." As one ancient writer puts it, people have "eternity in their hearts" but see only brevity and decay around them. Life is like a vapor.

***He has . . . set eternity in the hearts of men; yet they cannot fathom what God has done from beginning to end.***

**Ecclesiastes 3:11**

This came home to me when I was in the national archives in Canada doing doctoral research. I kept seeing a newspaper column from the 1970s by a guy who, apparently, had been a bigshot pundit. I had read dozens of books about Canada by that time, but I had never heard of this guy. He was a star in his day. He got invited to parties for big shots. But an eager and budding historian who was writing a dissertation on Canadian history had never heard of him. His hundreds of thousands of words had gone down the drain.

Not long after this I had a meeting with a member of Canada's Parliament. I walked out of the meeting feeling like I needed a shower. This guy was so hollow, so shallow, it astonished me that he could have been repeatedly elected to high office. Yet he could call the big newspapers anytime and get his name in print. He was on TV constantly. He met with world leaders.

Being a graduate student at the time I, of course, was wondering what I wanted to do when I grew up. I had this feeling that I wanted to be "important." But then I kept meeting people who held supposedly important jobs and I was unimpressed. Many of them seemed mediocre compared with other people I knew who were more talented and more deserving but weren't butt kissers, or they paid attention to students instead of hammering out academic articles no one would read (so they didn't get tenure), or they weren't slick and good at the networking game. All along, as I sat in classes taught by some mediocre, some good and some very good professors, I remembered that the best teacher I ever had taught at a nightmare of a high school and, at nights, at a no-name junior college.

All this pointed me to a basic fact—namely, that human life is ridiculous. Perhaps a better word is absurd. This claim makes many Christians (at least American Christians) nervous. They want to believe that if there is greater meaning in life than what we can create on our own, then life must make sense. But life doesn't make sense. I don't see how anyone could read the Bible and come away thinking that it paints a picture of a world that makes sense. If the idea that God came into the world via a teenage virgin living in a backwater of the Roman Empire isn't nutty, then I'm not sure what is.

This is one thing that I appreciate so much about the Bible. It takes seriously the fact that this world is nuts. The agony that pervades the natural world, the congenital geniuses in the Third World who never learn to read because their demonic governments don't care about them, restaurant workers on the upper floors of the World Trade Center forced to choose between jumping to their deaths or being immolated, Paris Hilton acquiring international fame while genuinely talented actors play bit parts in moldy theaters—all of this is crazy. And there's nothing I can think of in the Bible that suggests that someday good explanations for everything will be offered.

> ***"The foolishness of God is wiser than man's wisdom. The weakness of God is stronger than men's strength."***
>
> **St. Paul, 1 Corinthians 2:25 NIV**

You are right to criticize people who reject reality because they are waiting for everything to be made OK in the sweet by-and-by. There's nothing in the Bible to suggest that a good explanation will ever be offered for toddlers who die of cancer. I can't imagine hearing anything from any source that would make me say of a toddler's agony, "Oh, OK; now I get it. I see how little Johnny's pain made the world better."

But what's even worse is to see the door shut on Johnny's life and then to walk away from it saying that, in the end, everything—the life, the joy, the pain, the death—was meaningless except in a very limited sense. People know that some story is being worked out somehow and that, sadly, the story includes much pain. I want to know where this sense of things comes from. If it were just an idea passed on from generation to generation—if it didn't correspond to something inherent in people—it would have burned out, the way belief in Thor and Minerva has burned out.

So absurdity accompanies metaphysical meaning. This is a theme of Ecclesiastes and also of *Brideshead Revisited.* Resigned, skeptical, cynical and world-weary Charles Ryder goes through all that craziness—what he calls his "fierce little human tragedy"—but finds in the end that there was something to it: "I found it this morning, burning anew among the old stones."

It's easy to see how one would then go on to say that it's all also basically meaningless, that the only meaning to squeeze from life comes in day-to-day events and, one hopes, a sense at the end that one has done one's best. But I think that life is both absurd and meaningful. These two concepts aren't obvious chums, but there's tons of serious reflection on, and experience of, this phenomenon out there to suggest that today's ridiculous event is the precursor to tomorrow's big thing. I don't even think absurdity and meaning are paradoxical.

Now, I'm just a history teacher, so maybe what I'm going to write in the next few lines is bad theory, but it seems to me that the logic of any discussion of meaning has to start with the idea of extra-ordinary meaning. I notice that you, Albert Camus and John Kekes follow the same route: (1) You acknowledge that people have a desire for meaning, (2) for various reasons, you reject the idea of extra-ordinary meaning, and (3) all that's left is proximate meaning.

I don't know anyone who has consciously made the jump from (1) to (3) without pausing at (2)—as in, "I have a sense of purpose, and this can be satisfied by attending only to things I can see, touch, taste, smell or hear." Practically speaking, people live (1) and (3) lives—that is, they want to fit into some great and meaningful scheme; they want to be part of something worthwhile that's bigger than themselves. Even when a person decides that there is no ultimate meaning, the decision itself shows that thoughts about such a thing come naturally. This says something about the way people are wired.

I notice that you say in your dissertation (in the interview transcripts) and in some of your lyrics that you want evolution to become an epic or myth to replace the myths of old. So this is evolution as the Grand Story, the Answer. This certainly seems to be a reach for something beyond the mundane.

And I was struck by the many scientists you interviewed who were reluctant to dismiss the idea of things being beyond the reach of science. This quote from James Crow is fascinating:

> I don't know how to analyze [music] scientifically. I can certainly construct chords and do mathematics

in music, but that seems to be pretty far from the essence of it. Or poetry. . . . These are realms that, at least for the moment, are outside the realm of science. And yet, I don't want to say they're unreal.

A response could be that science will eventually make sense of these things, but that's a faith statement and so it doesn't add much clarity.

Well, I don't know if I've actually said anything. But this is one of the five directions my mind went in as I read your note.

All the best,
Preston

*Greg and Preston remain in touch. A brief exchange between them, written as the editing process was coming to an end, revealed that they were still at a friendly standoff.*

PJ: I've been editing all day. . . . I don't know where we found the time during those months to keep up the writing.

GG: Where did we find the time? You know the answer, my friend: The Lord works in mysterious ways!

### 1. Christianity and Violence

Several times in their correspondence, Greg and Preston consider the topic of violence done in the name of Christianity (see pages 133-36). Perhaps the greatest symbols of Christian violence are the witch trials of the early modern period. Below is a portion of a transcript of a witch trial that led to the torture and execution of a young French woman named Suzanne Gaudry.

> [Gaudry] says that . . . she is not a witch, and being a little stretched [on the rack] screams ceaselessly that she is not a witch, invoking the name of Jesus and Our Lady of Grace, not wanting to say any other thing.
>
> Asked if she did not confess that she had been a witch for twenty-six years.
>
> Says that she said it, [but] that she [now] retracts it, crying Jésus-Maria, that she is not a witch. . . .
>
> Suzanne Gaudry [is to be put] to death, tying her to a gallows, and strangling her to death, then burning her body and burying it there in the environs of the woods.

In his letters, Greg implies that violence and irrationality will decline to the extent that Christianity declines. The well-known evolutionary biologist Richard Dawkins makes the point this way:

> Religious beliefs are irrational. Religious beliefs are dumb and dumber: superdumb. Religion drives otherwise sensible people into celibate monasteries or crashing into New York skyscrapers. Religion motivates people to whip their own backs, to set fire to themselves or their daughters, [and] to denounce their own grandmothers as witches.

Preston acknowledges that much evil has been done in the name of Christianity, but argues that violence is hardly unique among Christians (or among religious people generally); it's a human problem, not a religious one. His view has been influenced by the moral philosopher John Kekes, who writes:

> The malevolent, selfish, cruel, fanatical motives we find in ourselves and the excessive rage, jealousy, or ambition we discover ourselves exhibiting are . . . unpleasant surprises. . . . We can blame the world, gods, conspirators, or civilization for causing disasters and injustices . . . but for the undeserved harm we cause, our own destructiveness is to be blamed.

### RESEARCH QUESTIONS

- What were the causes of the witch trials?
- What purpose did the people who put the witches on trial believe they were serving?
- Why had witch trials all but ended by the mid-eighteenth century?

### DISCUSSION QUESTIONS

- To what extent has Christianity been a force for harm? To

what extent has it been a force for good? On balance, has Christianity done more harm than good? What about secular ideologies?

- Would the world be better off if Christianity ceased to exist?
- Which claim better explains what we read in the first quote above, Dawkins's or Kekes's?

## 2. The Sense That There Is Something Else

A number of times Greg and Preston discuss whether it means anything that most people sense the presence of a spiritual world apart from, yet related to, this world (see pages 137-46). More than twenty years after the publication of his *Origin of Species*, Charles Darwin continued to think about this question, writing to a friend that he could "never make up [his] mind how far an inward conviction that there must be some Creator or First Cause is really trustworthy evidence."

Some who believe that this world is all there is recognize that this outlook can lead to pessimism. As the philosopher Jacques Monod wrote in the early 1970s, "The ancient covenant is in pieces; man at last knows that he is alone in the unfeeling immensity of the universe, out of which he emerged by chance."

Others, such as Cambridge University evolutionary paleobiologist Simon Conway-Morris, see the persistence of the feeling that there is "something more" as evidence that theology points people to something real. "The heart of the problem," Conway-Morris writes,

> is to explain how it might be that we, a product of evolution, possess an overwhelming sense of purpose and

> moral identity yet arose by processes that were seemingly without meaning. . . . Given that evolution has produced sentient species with a sense of purpose, it is reasonable to take the claims of theology seriously.

Still others who recognize that this sense exists are awed by the natural alone. Thus, Richard Dawkins writes:

> What I see in Nature is a magnificent structure that we can comprehend only very imperfectly, and that must fill a thinking person with a feeling of humility. This is a genuinely religious feeling that has nothing to do with mysticism.

### Research Questions

- What explanations do nontheists provide for the feeling most people have that there is more to life than this world?
- What explanations do Christian traditions provide for the sense that there is more to this life than this life?
- According to evolutionary theories, what role would such a feeling serve?
- According to Christian theories, what role does this feeling serve?

### Discussion Questions

- Why are many people depressed by the thought that there is nothing more than this life?
- Are Christian explanations plausible for the feeling that reality encompasses more than this world? Are nontheistic explanations plausible? Which seems more plausible?

## 3. Science and Christianity in Conflict

In his letters, Greg makes it clear that he sees no compatibility, in any traditional sense of the term, between a naturalistic worldview and Christianity (see pages 52-60). Indeed, the only religion he accepts as valid is one that "remains mute on the most meaningful matters of human experience, such as belief in gods, life after death, spirits, or souls." For Greg, a theological approach to these concepts is contradictory to a naturalistic worldview, partly because theological claims—i.e., "God loves people"—cannot be falsified using the scientific method.

The claims of Christianity provoke hostility from some scientists:

> Generally the state of mind of a believer in a revelation is the awful arrogance of saying, "I know, and those who do not agree with my belief are wrong." In no other field is such arrogance so widespread, in no other field do people feel so utterly certain of their "knowledge." It is to me quite disgusting that anybody should feel so superior, so selected and chosen against all the many who differ in their beliefs or unbeliefs.

This is not, however, the case among all scientists and evolutionists. Much "religious belief does not represent a form of mental weakness but rather the healthy functioning of the biologically and culturally well-adapted human mind," says David Sloan Wilson. And Harvard University zoologist Stephen Jay Gould writes:

> I do not see how science and religion could be unified,

> or even synthesized . . . but I also do not understand why the two enterprises should experience any conflict. Science tries to document the factual character of the natural world. . . . Religion, on the other hand, operates in an equally important, but utterly different, realm of human purposes, meanings and values—subjects that the factual domain of science might illuminate, but can never resolve.

The astronomer most associated with early conflict between Christianity and science, Galileo Galilei (1564-1642), also believed that faith and science led to different kinds of truth that emanated from a common source:

> I think that in discussions of physical problems we ought to begin not from the authority of scriptural passages, but from sense experiences and necessary demonstrations; for the holy Bible and the phenomena of nature proceed alike from the divine Word, the former as the dictate of the Holy Ghost and the latter as the observant executrix of God's commands.

### Research Questions

- Why has conflict often characterized the relationship between Christianity and science?
- How does the scientific method differ from the methods employed to gain theological knowledge?

### Discussion Questions

- Is conflict between Christianity and science necessary?

- Do you agree that people arrive at knowledge about the natural world and knowledge about God using different research methods? And must these forms of knowledge be kept separate?

## 4. Hating God

In one of his early notes, Preston writes that hatred of God, or of the idea of God, might be a kind evidence for God's existence (see page 32). Consider these words written by the protagonist Maurice Bendrix at the end of Graham Greene's novel *The End of the Affair:*

> I sat on my bed and said to God . . . You haven't got me yet. I know Your cunning. It's You who take us up to a high place and offer us the whole universe. You're a devil, God, tempting us to leap. But I don't want Your peace and I don't want Your love. . . . With Your great schemes You ruin our happiness as a harvester ruins a mouse's nest. I hate You, God, I hate You as though You existed.

Does it make sense to hate something that doesn't exist—to talk to something that doesn't exist?

A theme that runs through Greg's notes is that his negative reaction to the idea of God is really a response to the false, scientifically unverifiable or dubious beliefs people have defended in the name of God. In an interview with Greg, John M. Thoday of Cambridge University recalled:

> There came a time when I was about 16, when I read a hymn to myself that we were about to sing, and it said,

> "Lord we love thee. We deplore that we do not love thee more." And I said to myself, "Anybody who can write trite dreadful stuff like that, killing the English language, is unfit to talk to me." And I ceased to be religious for the rest of time.

Often, people reject the idea of God because they cannot understand how a Being that is omniscient and omnipotent could allow so much suffering in the world. In the Bad Religion song "God's Love," Greg sings:

> Tell me, where is the love?
> In a careless creation
> When there's no "above"
> There's no justice
> Just a cause and no cure
> And a bounty of suffering
> It seems we all endure

Honest Christian thinkers recognize that the problem of evil poses a serious challenge to the idea of an all-powerful, all-loving God. The physicist and theologian John Polkinghorne writes that

> when most people scan the world for signs of God it is not to its scientific orderliness that they look. Rather it is such matters as the incidence of debilitating and destructive disease that concern them. The randomly imposed burdens of unmerited suffering seem to many to call in question assertions that the world is in the care of a loving God.

How does Polkinghorne respond to this? He continues:

> At the deepest level I believe that the only possible answer is to be found in the darkness and dereliction of the cross, where Christianity asserts that in that lonely figure hanging there we see God himself opening his arms to embrace the bitterness of the strange world he has made.

### Research Questions

- Considering all branches of learning—literature, medicine, psychology and biology, for example—to what extent is Dawkins's claim justifiable that theology has made no significant contributions to knowledge?
- What have been the prominent theological responses to the problem of evil throughout Christian history?

### Discussion Questions

- What causes people to hate God? Does it make sense to hate the idea of a God that does not exist?
- Though many explanations for the problem of evil have been offered by theologians and philosophers, widespread suffering still blocks the way to belief in God for many people. Why do the answers to the problem of evil provided by theologians and philosophers seem inadequate to some people?

## 5. The Question of Meaning

Though thinking people who believe in God are able to provide kinds of evidence for God's existence, they are not able to prove God's existence the way they can prove, for example, that people need oxygen to survive. If a person were to doubt this claim, you would only need to take away his oxygen for a few seconds for him to change his mind. Some things are easy to prove.

But some important things are not so easy to prove. It is not easy to prove that life has meaning, and one observer has said that the "more the universe seems comprehensible, the more it also seems pointless."

What people usually mean when they say this is that life has no ultimate purpose. They do not believe in an afterlife, a next world, an answer to questions about why children die from cancer; they do not believe that history is moving in any predetermined direction; they do not believe that a wise Being presides over the world.

Clearly, though, most people do believe in ultimate purpose, even if they can't state exactly what that purpose is; to them, the idea that life is ultimately purposeless seems odd. To many people, the thought of an ultimately purposeless life is depressing. It is not depressing to everyone, however. As Greg writes:

> We can live with proximate purpose alone and still live fully satisfied lives without the mythology of ultimates. I believe humans would feel just as emotional and loving and caring in the absence of ultimates as they do going about carelessly thinking that a better world awaits them when they die. I think that we, like other social organisms, use proximate meaning and proximate purpose to get through life. Ultimates are an invention of theology, and one we cannot easily shake from our culture.

One has to wonder where humans would get a sense of ultimate purpose from a universe that is ultimately purposeless. Put another way, how could ultimate purposelessness produce feelings of ultimate purpose? Or do people mistake feelings of proximate purpose for something more than that? At the least, these questions place people in an awkward position vis-à-vis the universe they are part of. Considering this general theme in one of his notes to Greg, Preston asks:

> How can it make sense for people who are part of this "inevitable," impersonal, just-as-it's-supposed-to-be universe to want to change part of it, i.e., the behavior of others who are also part of the same universe? If we are really just a part of this impersonal universe and no more, then how would we know that something is wrong with the universe we're part and parcel of?

## Research Questions

- What explanations have been offered by professional scientists and philosophers who do not believe in ultimate purpose to make sense of this feeling most people have?
- What explanations have been offered by scientists, philosophers and theologians who do believe in ultimate purpose to account for the difficulty some people have in pinning down exactly what life's purpose is?

## Discussion Questions

- Do you sense that there is meaning to life that points to something beyond this life?

- Do you sense purpose in your life? If so, why? If not, why not?
- If you sense purpose in your life, is it linked to something greater than this life, or is it only concerned with this world?

# NOTES

*page 13* "I was working as a counselor": I've published a short article recounting some of my experiences working in a psychiatric ward. See "Crazy or Christian?" *Touchstone* 11, no. 3 (1998): 9-10.

*page 18* "In places like Olongapo": Preston Jones, "The Evil That We Do," Gravitas, winter 1997, p. 26.

*page 21* "Mediocre Minds": "Look around the country, an abundance you'll find of mediocre minds" (Greg Graffin, "Mediocre Minds," *No Substance* [1998]).

*page 23* "By the early 1980s": Preston Jones, "The Punk Rocker with a Ph.D.," *Books & Culture*, March/April 2004, p. 26.

*page 23* "Voracious March of Godliness": "But the missions were misguided and the trammeled led astray / The air resounds with thunder as the victors seized the day / And the haunting voice of history lives ignored but not betrayed / The voracious march of godliness will get us close to heaven one day" (Greg Graffin, "The Voracious March of Godliness," *No Substance* [1998]).

*page 24* "I don't know who Christopher Hitchens is": Hitchens's primary importance lies in his fierce intellectual independence. As a polemicist, he has no equal. A culture addicted to and daily manipulated by television could use more of his kind.

Certainly he has had low moments, such as *The Missionary Position* (1995), his sustained attack on Mother Teresa of Calcutta. But *No One Left to Lie To* (1999), an assault on President Bill Clinton, is unforgettable, as is his review of "public intellectual" Norman Podhoretz's memoir *Ex-Friends,* first published in *Harper's Magazine* in June 1999. Among other things, he calls Podhoretz a "crass power-worshiper whose only regrets are for himself, and who can conceive of no cause larger than his own esteem." Hitchens is an "anti-theist," but his temperament is that of an Old Testament prophet.

*page 25* "Christians need to be educated about the barbarism": Is Christianity dying? While the global population is growing by about 1.2 percent each year, the number of Christians worldwide is growing by 1.3 percent annually. This is about twice the yearly increase in the number of the world's atheists (.58 percent) and about one-third less that the annual growth in the number of Muslims (1.9 percent). Each year membership in Christian churches in Africa and Asia is growing by 2.36 percent and 2.64 percent, respectively. Church membership in Europe is declining by about .04 percent, though it is growing in the United States by nearly 1 percent annually.

*page 26* "At a provincial meeting": Robert Conquest, *Stalin: Breaker of Nations* (New York: Penguin Books, 1991), p. 213.

*page 27* "I saw that I should keep": Preston Jones, "History, Discernment and the Christian Life," in *The Best Christian Writing*, ed. John Wilson (San Francisco: HarperCollins, 2001), p. 162.

*page 27* "I was sitting": Christopher Hitchens, *Letters to a Young Contrarian* (Oxford: Perseus, 2001), p. 24.

*page 30* The local Catholic church: Since writing this, my wife and I have begun to attend an Episcopal church, though we know that given the divide between it and the global Anglican Communion, we will probably not be able to stay there.

*page 33* "I sat on my bed": Graham Greene, *The End of the Affair* (New York: Viking, 1951), p. 166.

*page 36* "I think naturalism fails": Interview with Gregory W. Graffin in "Evolution, Monism, Atheism and the Naturalist World-View" (Ph.D. diss., Cornell University, 2004), p. 239.

*page 38* "I have never found:" Quoted by Doug Van Pelt, *Rock Stars on God: 20 Artists Speak their Minds About Faith* (Lake Mary, Fla.: Relevant Books, 2004), p. 22.

*page 40* "Man's most sacred duty": Julian Huxley, *Religion Without Revelation* (New York: Harper & Brothers, 1957), p. 218.

*page 40* "The choice between": E. O. Wilson, *Consilience: The Unity of Knowledge* (New York: Alfred A. Knopf, 1998), p. 240.

*page 40* "History . . . reveals": Homer W. Smith, *Man and His Gods* (Boston: Little, Brown, 1952), p. 443.

*page 41* "In the case of living systems": Paul Davies, *God and the New*

*Physics* (New York: Touchstone, 1983), p. 62.

*page 44* "If all the achievements": Richard Dawkins, "On the Emptiness of Theology," *Free Inquiry* 18, no. 2 (1998): 6.

*page 46* "The world of today": Albert Camus, *Resistance, Rebellion and Death*, trans. Justin O'Brien (New York: Vintage, 1960), pp. 70-71.

*page 47* "The knowledge exists": Bertrand Russell, *Why I Am Not a Christian* (New York: Simon & Schuster, 1967), p. 47.

*page 48* "Human motives are mixed": John Kekes, *Moral Wisdom and Good Lives* (Ithaca, N.Y.: Cornell University Press, 1995), p. 68.

*page 50* "Where all are Christians": Søren Kierkegaard, *Attack upon "Christendom,"* trans. Walter Lowrie (Princeton, N.J.: Princeton University Press, 1968), pp. 27-28.

*pages 50-51* "Public confession is necessary": E. M. Zerr, "Confession," *Mission Messenger* 20, no. 11 (1958) <www.unity-in-diversity.org/MissionMessenger/vol20_1958/mm20_11b.html>.

*page 61* "our old neighborhood in the Valley": This is Southern Californian shorthand for the San Fernando Valley, made famous in the 1980s by Moon Zappa's song "Valley Girl."

*page 62* "If faith and reason": Kenneth R. Miller, *Finding Darwin's God: A Scientist's Search for Common Ground between God and Evolution* (New York: Harper Perennial, 2002), p. 267.

*page 63* "For all its objectivity": Simon Conway-Morris, *Life's Solution: Inevitable Humans in a Lonely Universe* (Cambridge: Cambridge University Press, 2003), p. 327.

*page 64* "Wind back the tape": Stephen Jay Gould, *Wonderful Life: The Burgess Shale and the Nature of History* (New York: W. W. Norton, 1989), pp. 14, 323.

*page 67* "What is good?": Friedrich Nietzsche, *The Twilight of the Idols and the Anti-Christ: or How to Philosophize with a Hammer*, trans. R. J. Hollingdale (New York: Penguin Classics, 1990), p. 127.

*page 69* "The human species": E. O. Wilson, *On Human Nature* (Cambridge, Mass.: Harvard University Press, 1978), p. 208.

*page 70* "If all people": James Q. Wilson, *The Moral Sense* (New York: Free Press, 1993), p. 196.

*page 71* "The terror of 1936-8": Robert Conquest, *Stalin: Breaker of*

*Nations* (New York: Penguin Books, 1991), p. 206.

*page 73* "Reality is a multi-layered unity": John Polkinghorne, *One World: The Interaction of Science and Theology* (Princeton, N.J.: Princeton University Press, 1989), p. 97.

*page 78* Discussion of the Fall: Among the many fine commentaries on the first chapters of Genesis is John C. Gibson, *Genesis,* vol. 1 (Philadelphia: Westminster Press, 1981).

*page 79* C. S. Lewis and David Lyle Jeffrey discuss the effects of the Fall: C. S. Lewis, *The Joyful Christian* (New York: Macmillan, 1977), p. 48; and David Lyle Jeffrey, *People of the Book: Christian Identity and Literary Culture* (Grand Rapids: Eerdmans, 1996), p. 144.

*page 81* "When most people": John Polkinghorne, *One World: The Interaction of Science and Theology* (Princeton, N.J.: Princeton University Press, 1989), p. 80.

*page 82* "The whole range": Cornelius Plantinga Jr., *Not the Way It's Supposed to Be: A Breviary of Sin* (Grand Rapids: Eerdmans, 1995), p. 2.

*page 85* "Our wealth is great": Wendell Berry, *Sex, Economy, Freedom and Community* (New York: Pantheon, 1993), pp. 73-74.

*page 86* "Even in its most basic form": Dennis Danielson, "Fall," in *A Dictionary of Biblical Tradition in English Literature*, ed. David Lyle Jeffrey (Grand Rapids: Eerdmans, 1992), p. 273.

*page 88* "In Niger": Todd Pitman, "Poverty in Niger worsened by other woes," *Arkansas Democrat-Gazette*, July 31, 2005, p. 17A.

*page 89* "I'm a theological 'libertarian' ": On the theological libertarian view, see William Hasker, *God, Time, and Knowledge* (Ithaca, N.Y.: Cornell University Press, 1989).

*page 89* "God bestows": Arthur R. Peacocke, "God's Interaction with the World: The Implications of Deterministic 'Chaos' and of Interconnected and Interdependent Complexity," in *Chaos and Complexity: Scientific Perspectives on Divine Action*, 2nd ed. (Tucson, Ariz.: Vatican Observatory Foundation, 2000), p. 281.

*page 92* "Brains evolved": Richard Dawkins, *The Blind Watchmaker: Why the Evidence of Evolution Reveals a Universe Without Design* (New York: Norton, 1996), pp. 157-58.

*page 97* "There is an intuition": Clark H. Pinnock, *Most Moved Mover:*

*A Theology of God's Openness* (Grand Rapids: Baker, 2001), pp. 160-61.

*page 101* "In crossing a heath": Quoted in Richard Swinburne, *Is There a God?* (Oxford: Oxford University Press, 1996), pp. 57-58.

*page 102* "Clutching children": "The Old Fire," Rimoftheworld.net, Oct. 24, 2004 <http://rimoftheworld.net/oldfireoneyear>.

*page 109* "Human beings": John Paul II, *Fides et Ratio: On the Relationship between Faith and Reason* (Boston: Pauline Books and Media, 1998), p. 42.

*page 114* "Here in the land of the free time": Greg Graffin, "The State of the End of the Millennium Address," *No Substance*, 1998.

*page 114* "We justified the world": Dietrich Bonhoeffer, *The Cost of Discipleship* (New York: Touchstone, 1995), pp. 53-54.

*page 115* "Poor Sebastian!": Evelyn Waugh, *Brideshead Revisited* (New York: Penguin Books, 1951), pp. 351-52.

*page 117* "Our evolution didn't hinge": Greg Graffin, "Raise Your Voice," *No Substance*, 1998.

*page 127* "*Da mihi*": Augustine *The Confessions* 1:1. Preston Jones's translation.

*page 132* "Believing that there is not a god": Interview with Gregory W. Graffin in "Evolution, Monism, Atheism and the Naturalist World-View" (Ph.D. diss., Cornell University, 2004), p. 178.

*page 133* "Perhaps, child brains": Ibid., pp. 120-21.

*page 136* "Forty-five years ago Quebecers": See Preston Jones, "Quebec *Indépendentisme* and the Life of Faith," *Journal of Church and State* 43, no. 2 (2001): 251-65.

*pages 145-46* "I don't know how": Interview with Gregory W. Graffin in "Evolution, Monism, Atheism and the Naturalist World-View" (Ph.D. diss., Cornell University, 2004), p. 210.

*page 147* "[Gaudry] says that": Katharine Lualdi, ed., *The Making of the West*, vol. 2 (Boston: Bedford/St. Martin's, 2005), pp. 39-40.

*page 148* "Religious beliefs are irrational": Richard Dawkins, "Atheists for Jesus," *Free Inquiry* 25, no. 1 (2004-2005): 9.

*page 148* "The malevolent, selfish, cruel": John Kekes, *Facing Evil* (Princeton, N.J.: Princeton University Press, 1990), p. 29.

*page 149* "Never make up [his] mind": Quoted in Janet Browne, *Charles Darwin: The Origin and After—the Years of Fame* (New York: Alfred A. Knopf, 2002), p. 391.

*page 149* "The ancient covenant": Quoted in John Polkinghorne, *One*

*World: The Interaction of Science and Theology* (Princeton, N.J.: Princeton University Press, 1989), p. 53.

*pages 149-50* "The heart of the problem": Simon Conway-Morris, *Life's Solution: Inevitable Humans in a Lonely Universe* (Cambridge, U.K.: Cambridge University Press, 2003), pp. 2, 328.

*page 150* "What I see in Nature": Richard Dawkins, "Religion-Einsteinian or Supernatural?" *Free Inquiry* 24, no. 2 (2004): 9.

*page 151* "Remains mute on the most meaningful matters": Gregory W. Graffin, "Evolution, Monism, Atheism and the Naturalist World-View" (Ph.D. diss., Cornell University, 2004), pp. 97-98.

*page 151* "Generally the state of mind of a believer": H. Bondi quoted in Paul Davies, *God and the New Physics* (New York: Touchstone, 1983), p. 6.

*page 151* "Much 'religious belief' ": David Sloan Wilson, *Darwin's Cathedral: Evolution, Religion, and the Nature of Society* (Chicago: University of Chicago Press, 2003), p. 228.

*pages 151-52* "I do not see how science and religion": Stephen Jay Gould, *Rocks of Ages: Science and Religion in the Fullness of Life* (New York: Ballantine, 1999), p. 4.

*page 152* "I think that in discussions of physical problems": Galileo's letter to the Grand Duchess Christina of Tuscany, in Katharine Lualdi, ed., *The Making of the West,* vol. 2 (Boston: Bedford/St. Martin's, 2005), p. 33.

*page 153* "I sat on my bed": Graham Greene, *The End of the Affair* (New York: Viking, 1951), p. 166.

*pages 153-54* "There came a time when I was about 16": Gregory W. Graffin, "Evolution, Monism, Atheism and the Naturalist World-View" (Ph.D. diss., Cornell University, 2004), p. 184.

*pages 154-55* "when most people scan": John Polkinghorne, *One World: The Interaction of Science and Theology* (Princeton, N.J.: Princeton University Press, 1989), p. 80.

*page 156* "The 'more the universe seems comprehensible' ": Steven Weinberg quoted in Paul Davies, *God and the New Physics* (New York: Touchstone, 1983), p. 44.

**Preston Jones** grew up in Southern California, served in the U.S. Navy from 1986-1990 and now teaches history and Latin at John Brown University. He has published over two hundred articles in general and academic publications, and he is a contributing editor to *Books & Culture* and *Critique*. He runs one or two marathons a year.

**Greg Graffin** is the singer and songwriter for the band Bad Religion. He holds a master's degree in geology from UCLA and a Ph.D. in zoology from Cornell University. His favorite professional activity is weaving scientific ideas and their implications into provocative songs with catchy melodies. His dissertation, "Evolution, Monism, Atheism and the Naturalist World-View," is available at <www.polypterus.org>. Bad Religion's official website is <www.badreligion.com>. Greg's second solo CD is *Cold as the Clay*.